JEFFREY D. WILHELM

Enriching Comprehension
WITH
Visualization Strategies

Text Elements and Ideas
to Build Comprehension,
Encourage Reflective Reading,
and Represent Understanding

■■SCHOLASTIC

NEW YORK • TORONTO • LONDON • AUCKLAND • SYDNEY
MEXICO CITY • NEW DELHI • HONG KONG • BUENOS AIRES

Dedication

This effort is dedicated to five special friends,
thinking partners, and teachers:

Bill Bedford, the Wachsmeister
Paul Corrigan, the Old Animal
Bruce Hunter, the Counselor
Sandip Wilson, the Great-Hearted
Willie Stewart, the Coach

You live out loud
and teach by letting your lives speak.
You make visible what you believe and how to live.
You inspire me and I am grateful.

Cover and Interior Designer: Maria Lilja
Copy/Production Editor: Danny Miller
Cover photograph by Maria Lilja
Interior photographs on page 7 by Jane Buchbinder; and pages 27, 31, and 178 by Michael C. York
Page 112,L: American Gothic by Grant Wood. Gift of Friends of the American Art Collection. All rights reserved by the Art Institute of Chicago and VAGA, New York, NY. Image of "American Gothic" supplied by Corbis.
Page 112,R: Gas Mask Gothic by Richard Hess. Used by permission of HessDesignWorks.com.
Page 149,L: Doug Berry/iStockphotography, page 149,R: pafe/iStockphotography
All other interior photographs by Karen Baicker

ISBN: 978-0-545-21884-9

1 2 3 4 5 6 7 8 9 10 23 19 18 17 16 15 14 13 12

Contents

Acknowledgments

In the National Writing Project, we refer to ourselves as "thinking partners." Fortunately, my life is filled with the special kinds of teachers who can be called thinking partners—or brave companions, teammates, or helpmates. Over the past several years, as my wife has struggled with a rare vascular disease and I have undertaken the challenge to balance responsibilities and projects, I have never been more cognizant and grateful for everyone who is a thinking and living partner through daily challenges and over time.

Whenever I have cause to reflect about such relationships, as when I write the acknowledgments for a project such as this book, I'm truly humbled by the recognition of how much I have been assisted and how much I have learned from my family, friends, students, and fellow teachers. Teachers are those who see us through our life challenges. Anne Lamott writes, "We are not here to see through one another, but to see one another through." The following people have done just that for me. It would be impossible for me to thank everyone who deserves it, but I will try to mention just a few of those who deserve a most special thanks.

Heartfelt gratitude goes to Sandip Wilson for taking time out of her busy schedule on several occasions to read this manuscript and for giving me many most excellent suggestions. Rachel Bear provided invaluable help in many ways, particularly with ideas for meeting the Common Core State Standards (CCSS) through visual strategies. Many thanks to Erika Boas for her help as a thinking partner about many interesting teaching challenges and the practicalities of meeting them. Karl Androes, director of Whirlwind and the Reading in Motion program in Chicago, also read drafts and made helpful suggestions. I'm also grateful to my friends Mary Massie and Karen Boran from the Chicago Teaching Center, and to the rest of the CTC crew, for their brave forays into arts education. Many of their tips and insights helped to seed and extend the work that is reported here.

My heartfelt appreciation and thanks go to my wife, Peggy Jo Wilhelm, teacher extraordinaire and my first reader and editor of every draft, and to Tanya Baker, my long-time thinking partner, for contributions too numerous to mention.

I would not be a teacher, nor a writer, except for the influence of my friend and mentor Michael W. Smith, the esteemed researcher George Hillocks, and my own high school English teachers Bill Strohm and James Blaser, who made me see that teaching is among the most complex, challenging, fulfilling, and worthwhile of life pursuits.

To my many colleagues and friends, I blow my trumpet and raise my sword in a sincere salute. Thanks go to my colleagues at Boise State University, who have helped me adjust to a new professional situation, particularly Bruce Ballenger, Jim Fredricksen, Bruce Robbins, and Stan Steiner. My thanks to my colleagues and friends in the Maine Writing Project and the National Writing Project, where so many of the best teaching ideas take shape and are shared. And I am constantly cognizant of the continued collegiality of old—or should I say "longstanding" mentors and teaching partners, like Brian Ambrosius, Erv Barnes, Bill Bedford, Ed Brazee, Paul Corrigan, Mike Ford, Paul Friedemann, Stuart Greene, Leon Holley, Jr., Bruce Hunter, Jan Kristo, Craig Martin, Paula Moore, Bruce Nelson, Bruce Novak, Wayne Otto, John Thorpe, Sandip Wilson, Brian White, and Denny Wolfe. And of course an extra dose of gratitude to my hard-headed, tough-minded, and entirely loving family, particularly my wife, Peggy Jo; and the most amazing teachers of my life journey: my daring and sometimes dutiful daughters, warriors of faith, lovers of living life to the fullest, Fiona Luray and Jasmine Marie.

In writing this book, I've gleaned ideas from over 30 years of classroom teaching and professional sharing. I've tried my best to trace the provenance of various notions to particular teachers and students but welcome any emendations for those I may have missed.

Author's Note: Visualization Strategies and the Common Core State Standards

In my opinion, the Common Core State Standards (CCSS) offer the best opportunity for progressive educational change that I have seen in more than 30 years as an educator. Using visualization strategies to promote more proficient reading, composing, and learning across topics, themes, and genres has never been more important. The CCSS represent a welcome and profound paradigm shift towards instruction that focuses on student expertise and the strategic tools that they need to excel across the disciplines.

Please note that these standards cannot be addressed, much less met, through business as usual. The standards call on every teacher to transform his or her teaching into a problem-oriented, meaning-making pursuit that develops effective strategic capacities. A robust body of research shows that developing strategic knowledge requires modeling, mentoring, and monitoring students' use of strategies in meaningful contexts—and how to do so is a major theme of the first few chapters of this book.

Look at the language of the CCSS: the standards use active production verbs such as *write*, *produce*, *research*, *argue*, and *persuade*. The later chapters of this book include engaging ideas for collaborative inquiry projects, opportunities for students to use technology and multimedia, and ways that you can draw on both formative and summative assessment to monitor and track your students' progress with Common Core and more (watch for the CCSS icons in the margins signaling a direct link). The comprehension and composition strategies I introduce in this book are useful in helping students to succeed as proficient, independent readers and composers of high quality, complex text.

Embracing the standards doesn't mean abandoning our smart, principled approach to informed teaching. What we know about time-tested research, best practices, and, particularly, those specific human beings who are our own students remains as critical as ever. Did you know that in a typical fourth-grade classroom, you're likely to find a reading span of seven grades—from a second-grade reading level all the way to ninth-grade ability (Hargis, 2006)? Clearly, one size does not fit all. It makes sense, then, to provide our students with as many possible ways to access, comprehend, and converse with challenging texts of all kinds. Our struggling readers and writers, Limited Formal Schooling (LFS) students, and English Language Learners will succeed to the extent that we scaffold and differentiate our instruction.

Finally, the Common Core State Standards call for making our classrooms arenas of productivity and creativity (instead of consumption) where students may produce written work across genres, dramatic and theatrical performances, and create a wide range of artifacts from videos to museum exhibits. We need to move from places where kids only consume other people's meanings to places where they create their own.

This book will help you develop a productive repertoire of diverse teaching and learning strategies; what's more, you'll learn what contexts and strategies work best to assist students in becoming proficient readers and composers. Above all, you will promote a dynamic mindset (Dweck, 2009) of growth and potential in both your students and yourself that will lead to a lifetime of productive learning.

—Jeff Wilhelm
Boise, Idaho, July 2012

Introduction

My wife has a rare vascular disorder and has suffered several severe brain bleeds that have caused substantial brain damage. She lost her capacity to read, to read music (she was a professional musician and music methods professor), and her capacity to identify and reason with many concepts. Her therapists used versions of many of the visual strategies featured in this book to help her regain all of these capacities. Because of her condition, I have read widely on neuroplasticity and the brain. One book that I quite like is John Medina's *Brain Rules* (2008). He cites 12 rules about the brain to remember when you are learning. The ninth is sensory integration: stimulate more of the senses. "Multisensory learning means better remembering and deeper understanding." Rule #10 is vision: vision trumps all other senses. It is the most powerful means to learning—which has both costs and many benefits—most of which we neglect to leverage in schools. Though my personal situation is somewhat unique, it does highlight the power of visualization in teaching both concept and process with all learners, particularly with those who struggle in some way.

I first came to utilize visualization strategies to teach through my intervention efforts to assist struggling upper elementary and middle school readers back in the late eighties and early nineties. In my research for *You Gotta BE the Book* (Wilhelm, 1997/2008), I found how multifarious and marvelous these kinds of visual strategies are for helping students not only to develop "constrained" skills (skills that are necessary but once mastered do not offer any additional benefits) such as decoding and "unconstrained" strategies (i.e., strategies like inferencing and others that can be developed with exponentially developing pay-offs throughout a lifetime) associated with comprehension, interpretation, response, justified thinking, and deep understanding. In addition to teaching students "how" to master a wide variety of unconstrained strategies, many visual techniques help students to understand data, to turn information into concepts, to think and argue with data and concepts, to make new connections, and to compose new meanings in a variety of genres.

Anchor Standards for Writing, 1, 2

Anchor Standards for Reading, 1–9

All of these are essential elements of the Common Core State Standards, Anchor Standards, and Standards for Literacy in the Disciplines. Since those days in the early nineties, I've come to appreciate visual strategies even more. I've used them in my own teaching of science, social studies, and literacy, and worked with teachers from early elementary through college to incorporate them into instruction to promote both literacy in terms of reading and writing/composing, and to achieve deep understanding in all content areas.

To view a sample of the widely varying visualization techniques and their uses, point your Web browser to www.visual-literacy.org/periodic_table/periodic_table.html By mousing over the different cells, you will access examples and explanations of each featured technique. This "periodic table" is designed to help students "evaluate, apply, or create conceptual visual representations." In this book, I will explore mostly how to use these kinds of visuals as a support in developing

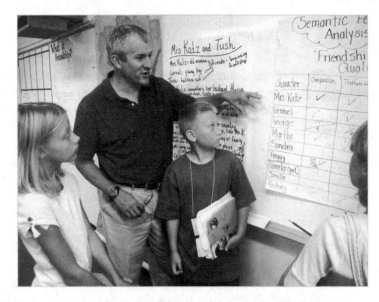

Jeff works with third graders to create a Semantic Feature Analysis to help them define friendship.

procedures of literate practice—through both constrained and unconstrained strategies associated with reading. I will also allude to how these techniques will help learners to understand and compose about their emerging understandings in ways consistent with this periodic table. I have found the table to be extremely useful, but not comprehensive. Many visual techniques, including quite a few from this book, are not included, such as, ironically, the technique of creating a periodic table!

The use of a variety of such rich visual techniques to promote better reading and composing, deeper understanding, and more adept application may be rewarded more at this moment than at any other time in my teaching career. At the time of this writing, 46 states have endorsed the new Common Core State Standards (CCSS) and more than 40 have legislated their implementation. This represents what I find to be a hugely welcome but also profound paradigm shift that will offer many new but appropriate challenges to teachers and students alike. One of my current worries is that teacher leaders will try to show how current curriculum and instruction already meet the CCSS (which traditional methods and materials most decidedly do not) instead of taking a historical opportunity to reframe what we do to professionalize teaching and work for the benefit of our students.

For example, the CCSS are entirely procedural—emphasizing the processes and strategies of comprehending, making meaning, interpreting, reflecting, justifying, critiquing, and the achieving of deep understanding that I have found visualization strategies so powerful at in helping students to develop. Actual content knowledge is almost entirely undefined, since to use procedures students must develop deep conceptual knowledge as a natural matter of course. A robust body of research shows that developing procedural knowledge requires modeling, mentoring, and monitoring students' actual use of strategies in meaningful contexts of use (how to do so is a major theme of the first few chapters of this book).

Text Complexity Standards

Procedural knowledge is what students need to become autonomous problem-solvers addressing the evolving and ever-changing issues in their own lives and the world. In addition, the CCSS for text complexity are higher than anything yet seen, without allowances for struggling readers or ELLs or LFS students. Again, I am very impressed with these standards—in my opinion, they offer the best chance for progressive educational change that I have seen in over 30 years as an educator. The standards align nicely with what we know about learning from cognitive science and about literacy from educational research.

However, it must be stressed that these standards cannot be addressed, much less met, through business as usual; in other words, in the typical ways in which American educators regard and practice teaching as the purveying of information. A much more vital and assistive and strategic kind of work must be undertaken in classrooms for these standards to be met. Every teacher of every kind of student will be called upon to transform their teaching into problem-oriented meaning-making kinds of pursuits that develop new procedural capacities. To meet the text-complexity standards, students will have to be met in their "zone of proximal development" and helped to continually outgrow their current capacities. This will require the differentiation of reading materials, methods, grouping, layers of instructional support and more. Inquiry, defined as the rigorous apprenticeship into expertise, is the instructional model most conducive to differentiation and to the achievement of real-world expertise. These assertions are explored here in the early chapters, and more fully in my book *Engaging Readers and Writers with Inquiry* (Wilhelm, 2007).

Not only have I used visualization strategies (and worked with a wide variety of teachers using them) to help struggling readers and writers, but I've also used them with students more adept in their literacy to continuously improve their reading, composing, and understanding.

This past year, I co-taught an AP English class with Rachel Bear, a fantastic young teacher and the leader of the Boise State Writing Project CCSS Implementation team. We used a wide variety of visual techniques in our teaching. In one unit that explored the essential question "What are the costs and benefits of technology?" Rachel used a PowerPoint presentation of famous scientists and the various results of their work (e.g., Oppenheimer and the atomic bomb) to get students inferencing and debating the different and potentially beneficial and deleterious effects of recent technological advances. In another unit, organized around the essential question "What work does 'funny' do?" students were asked to post on our class wiki various "texts," including visual and multimodal ones, that they found "funny." Students were then asked to read each other's posts and rank them. This led to a visual scheme classifying different kinds of humorous texts (pastiche, satire, irony, misdirection jokes, slapstick, etc.) and the work that each one did. In both cases, we made use of visuals to "frontload" the students' enthusiasm and background knowledge, and prepare them for success with very substantive work.

I also work closely with Erika Boas, a highly energetic and creative teacher who is a Boise State Writing Project (BSWP) International fellow from Hobart, Tasmania. This past year, Erika has used visuals such as flow charts and timelines as kinds of process analyses to help her students describe and justify their problem-solving procedures and conclusions. This kind of metacognitive reflection is required by the CCSS and the Smarter Balance and PARCC Assessments. Much of this learning has occurred in a Studies of Society and History class where Erika aimed to use visualization strategies as a way to help her students understand big concepts, learn new procedures for learning, and be accountable for and to share what they had learned.

Erika used visualization tools and strategies to aid her students in reading comprehension in the context of both her English and History classes. In Writers' Workshop, Erika worked with students to generate and shape material in their compositions through the use of visual strategies.

Though I will explore the advantages of teaching with visual techniques throughout this book, it's worth citing some of the ones up front that will help us meet the CCSS and the current challenges facing our students.

Visual Strategies:

- are great fun and particularly motivating and useful for students who might be labeled struggling or English Language Learners (ELLs), Limited English Proficiency (LEP), or Limited Formal Schooling (LFS).

- are active and engaging for everyone in the class and provide communal and shareable experiences for different kinds of students.

- offer safe ways to try out new strategies and to share evolving understandings.

- lead to deep, justified, and substantive learning.

- are interactive and democratic, offering powerful forms of joint productive activity as described by Vygotsky.

- promote deep understanding and use of practically any concept or strategy, genre structure, or language convention since every reading strategy promoted by visualization is also an inquiry strategy.

- foster the forces of imagination, creativity, and problem-solving that are rarely unleashed in schools.

- are important to multimodal reading and composing (required by the CCSS), as well as most digital composing.

- provide compelling ways to create "design" projects analogous to what experts create and that are the end of all inquiry.

- are practically foolproof. Visual strategies work, but are rarely used in schools to promote the deep procedural and conceptual learning that are the aim of this book. The students become enthusiastic co-producers of curriculum and meaning, so the activities are spontaneous and energizing and growth-inducing.

For your convenience, the text in the following chapters is coded with icons referring you to particular examples from the DVD.

This second edition includes Frequently-Asked Question (FAQs) about visualization and a section on how to use technology to promote and extend the visualization strategy repertoire. It also includes a DVD, filmed during a National Writing Project "Camp Reading Rocks" for kids—many of whom are ELLs, LFS students, or struggling readers. What you will see in the DVD are real teachers using visual strategies for the first time with real kids. The DVD will show you how you can reasonably introduce some of the techniques with your own students to various ends. Once you start using visual techniques, I have no doubt that you will develop many original and hybridized versions of your own in service of your own students' specific needs. For your convenience, the text is coded with icons referring you to particular examples from the DVD.

If you'd like to see more video clips of me explaining a range of comprehension strategies and learning theory, check out the Curriculum Services of Canada (CSC): curriculum.org/content/about-csc. Type "Jeff Wilhelm" into the search line and a complete offering of my archived webcasts will pop up; it's all free—download and enjoy.

Finally, this book will tell two stories. The first is how I came to use this process of showing/helping/letting go as I developed and adapted visual strategies to assist my students in their reading. These techniques have been particularly effective for helping my struggling readers, but as I will show, they have powerful effects for all readers, including accomplished ones.

The second story, which runs like an undercurrent through this book, is of my ongoing and ever-evolving journey to become a better teacher. This story is about my realization that whenever I did improve my practice, it was because I responded reflectively to a challenge thrown out to me by my students, because of a failure of my teaching, or because of a set of problems I wasn't adequately addressing or solving. In other words, here is a story of how I learned from my students how to teach them more responsively and effectively.

FREQUENTLY-ASKED QUESTIONS ABOUT VISUALIZATION STRATEGIES

The Why, When, and How

It was lunchtime. I was sitting at my desk in the empty classroom grading a few last papers when Curtis walked in. Curtis was a bit of a ragamuffin, dressed mostly in blaze orange, and sporting a thick mop of curly brown hair. He was a friendly troublemaker, and struggled with reading and the rest of school despite possessing some obvious smarts. I liked him a lot. "Curtis!" I called. "What's up?"

He meandered across the room and deposited himself heavily on the couch next to my desk.

"Ya know, Mr. Wilhelm," he offered. "School just isn't about the kids anymore."

"How's that?" I asked.

"Teachers just give you a bunch of stuff to do and never help you. And they don't care what you can do or what

First Deer

In that thicket of creaking firs,
my sleeves rolled up, the cold
stropping its frosty blade on my spine,
I unlocked the warmth of a deer.
The sweet reek of his cedar-filled
    paunch
scented the air as my father,
placing his hands on mine,
guided them to the warm, wet heart.
And as we felt under the hide, touching
the lungs and the stout cord of the
    windpipe,
he'd tell me what they were,
for he was pleased with this first deer
his boy had killed with one shot
through a screen of green growth.
He'd shot so many it tickled him
to see the thrill renewed in me
as I shivered with awe
and a little regret and winced
when I caught a whiff from the gut
or felt the hot blood trickle down my
    arm.
And as we worked on into dusk
without even checking a watch,
I thought of that quiet moment at mass
when the altar boy and the priest
get together to wash the chalice
and return the host to its house of gold,
unconcerned with who's looking on,
heads bent, eyes lowered, making sure
they clean everything up.
Then father flung the young nub horn
across his shoulders and struck off
while I tripped along behind him
until we reached camp in the dark
where we hung the carcass to drain
and went in to warm our bellies
with coffee, fried liver, and heart.

—PAUL CORRIGAN

you are interested in. They don't pay any attention to the kids: they just give out the work. Why is it that someone who doesn't even know us says what kids are supposed to do?"

I wasn't sure what brought on this philosophical lament, and Curtis wasn't offering any specifics. So to change the subject, and maybe even find out more by changing the mood, I picked up a poetry book by my friend Paul Corrigan.

"Curtis, I know you like hunting. So I'd like your opinion of this poem. Come on over beside me so we can read it together."

I read the poem "First Deer" aloud, about Paul's first hunting trip with his father.

"See!" Curtis said excitedly when I'd finished. "That's just what I mean! That dad in the poem helped his son see what to do, and then he helped him do it so he could see and feel and know how to do it on his own. They worked together! That's how my pops taught me to hunt, too. But they don't do that for you in school."

Show me how. This is what Curtis wanted from me. I couldn't help but feel that he had come to me to ask for help with his reading. And the trust he placed in me made me feel an awesome responsibility.

One of the ways I was able to help Curtis during that school year was through the use of visualization strategies, which show kids how to become better readers by making the elements and strategies of the reading process visible, concrete, and available to them. And in the same way that the father in Corrigan's poem shows his son how to gut a deer by first literally guiding his son's hands, I have tried to teach Curtis and other students over the years in a manner that keeps in sight a novice's need to be supported before working on his or her own.

Frequently-Asked Questions About Visualization Strategies

Over the years, in my visualization workshops and in email exchanges with teachers across the country, I've collected a list of recurring questions about visualization techniques. Here are the most popular FAQs—and answers to them, too, of course!

Why do you think this visualization stuff is so important anyway?

Research in literacy shows that whenever engaged and competent readers are reading they create intense visualizations in their mind. When reading both fictional and nonfictional narratives this can be called a "story world" or "secondary world" that the reader creates in concert with the text, enters, and moves around in. Even with explanatory/informational or argument texts, adept readers create mental models of the text, its structure, and of the concepts under consideration. One of the most fundamental differences between good and poor readers is that poor readers do not visualize to make meaning while they read. Bottom line: readers who do not "see" what they read cannot be said to be reading at all. (See Wilhelm, 1995; 1997/2008 for full discussions.)

Q&A I: What is visualization technique and how does it support students to read with understanding?

Likewise, research in cognition demonstrates that when we "understand" we have a "dual processing model" in place (Paivio, 1986). We can explain what we understand and how we have come to understand it, but we also have a visual understanding of what we know and how we know it. So to achieve, represent, share, and use deep procedural and/or conceptual understanding, we need to visualize. Students who do not visualize when they read need to be helped to do so. That is the purpose of this book.

Anchor Standards for Writing, I–3

Anchor Standards for Speaking and Listening, I–5

Anchor Standards for Reading, I–9

Particularly given the evolving multimodal nature of text and the new CCSS standards for reading, writing, and literacy in the disciplines, giving students visual tools for reading, composing, and understanding process, craft, and text structure has become even more important.

What are visual tools and in what ways are they used to promote literacy?

A tool is anything that develops and extends human capacity. In this book, visual tools are those that students can use to promote their learning of any process of reading, composing, speaking or listening, or of any concept that they are reading about. Visual tools are also hugely helpful in developing, organizing, composing, and representing what has been learned.

The tools presented here can be prosthetics for helping students develop constrained skills like alphabetic or phonemic awareness, or decoding, or any unconstrained skill like using images in different ways to help students visualize and comprehend or to engage in any process of reading related to comprehension, response, interpretation, or critique of what has been learned. A visual tool can also involve images, graphics, and graphic organizers that assist students to place-hold, organize, analyze, and synthesize what they have read or learned. Such tools are also on point for representing, sharing, and archiving what has been learned in visual or multimodal forms. As such, visual tools are essential to all processes of understanding and of inquiry itself.

Visualization Tips

How can the use of art or visuals lead to substantive learning about literacy or in the content areas?

Visual tools and supports have been shown to help students master processes of constrained skills like alphabetic and phonemic awareness as well as decoding. Even more powerful, visual tools and artwork have important effects on promoting unconstrained strategies related to comprehension, such as activating background knowledge, making inferences and seeing connections, critiquing and evaluating, interpreting and responding, demonstrating, and representing.

Beyond these kinds of general processes of reading or composing, visuals are also powerful for developing task and text specific tools. In fact, I don't know of a process or genre that can't be taught using visual tools such as cartoons. For example, see *Fresh Takes on Teaching the Literary Elements* (Smith and Wilhelm, 2010) for a complete discussion on how comics can teach the reading and writing of different genres including the text-specific processes necessary to the mastery of reading and writing in each genre.

Visual tools are also powerful in developing and consolidating conceptual understandings. Picture maps and culminating projects like video documentaries make students accountable for their learning in actual accomplishment and performances such as those that are used in the world beyond school.

Visual tools and artwork also have many personal internal benefits. Artistic response can act as a "transitional object" that helps a student to outgrow her current self, helping to safely navigate a zone of proximal development that may be procedural, conceptual, or even emotional and psychological. For a full discussion of this use of art, see *Teaching Literacy for Love and Wisdom* (Wilhelm and Novak, 2011).

When should teachers use visual strategies?

JIT, PON, WA, DIY—that is, "just in time," at the "point of need," "when appropriate," and in service of "doing it yourself." Like any tool kit, the tools should be brought out only when there is some work for which he tool is appropriate. I often see my student teachers use a visual tool like it's a trick from a grab bag—they think it will be fun to do and that it will work to engage their students. This makes visual activities a kind of "throwaway" instead of a powerful tool for consciously promoting deeper capacities and understanding. I push myself and the teachers with whom I work to develop more "conscious competence" in considering what their students need to learn right now, and what they need to know next and be able to do in order to accomplish a significant task currently just beyond their reach (i.e., in their ZPD). Then I ask them to consider what tools in their repertoire—whether think-alouds, dramas, or visual tools—would be best suited to meet these immediate needs and contribute to students' evolving understandings, helping them to develop the capacities necessary to demonstrate their understanding on culminating projects that address the inquiry topic under consideration.

Q&A 3: How do visualization strategies help students build background knowledge before and during reading?

I'm personally not very artistic, so how can I model how to use these strategies? And what about kids who are not very artistic either?

This is an easy one. I'm personally not very artistic. But this hasn't stopped me from using visual tools. Magazines and online images are easy to find and use in conjunction with visual strategies. Likewise, computer-generated images are easy to create. Sometimes I ask students to compose with their off-hand, or use Brian Andreas's "naïve artwork" as models to downplay the notion that the work has to look refined.

Here's another thing. I tell my students that everybody gets to do some of what they are good at. For lots of my students, particularly those labeled as LD, visual learning is one of their strengths. Accessing and using their strengths is fun, identifies them as competent, and gives them a resource to address their weaknesses. And that is how we learn, by using our strengths and current capacities to learn new capacities and develop new strengths. I also tell my students that everybody has to do some of what they are not good at. That's because learning is about taking on challenges and becoming stronger and more facile, building an ever-expanding repertoire. I tell my students that if they are good at something, they need to find people to help become good at this, too. And if they are struggling with something, they need to find someone to help them improve. This is an argument for a democratic classroom. Everyone gets to use their strengths and apply them to the common project. Likewise, we all have to help each other to get better and stronger as a problem-solving community.

I have found that when the process is purposeful and assisted, students almost always like to work together, to help each other learn, and to learn from each other.

DVD

Q&A 4:
Should visualization strategies be individualized for students or do the same strategies work for all learners?

How will visual strategies help students to meet the Common Core State Standards (CCSS) and other learning objectives?

The CCSS are almost entirely procedural. That is, they are about developing profoundly important strategies for reading, writing, speaking, listening, and learning. The CCSS gives lots of attention to rhetorical choices, text structure, and the use of various conventions for specific meanings and effects. Visual strategies are particularly good for developing just these kinds of procedural tools, as will be seen throughout the book. As cognitive science has shown, visual models and processes are extremely powerful ways of navigating one's zone of proximal development.

How can you go about assessing this kind of visual work?

I'd like to make an important distinction here between informal practice, in which the teacher and the environment provide assistive support versus formal final projects, in which the teacher moves from being coach to referee and from advocate to judge. This highlights the distinction between formative assessment for learning and summative assessment of learning.

When students are learning a new set of strategies or concepts, we need to assist them and give them lots of assisted practice. Through this process we need to provide formative assessments that give continual supportive feedback about what needs to be tackled next. Only when they have the requisite practice for mastery should students be given a summative assessment or evaluation. I must add that I believe it unethical to grade students on something you haven't taught them and helped them to know how to do over time. The use of visual strategies throughout a unit are rehearsals: they are meant to provide practice in using a new sophisticated strategy and in dealing with new and difficult concepts. Recent research in cognition has shown how important both multimodality and repeated practice are to mastering and consolidating new kinds of learning. Throughout a unit, I typically provide feedback and award points for completion of daily "deliverables." The points are given for effort, completion, or improvement. The visual activities themselves can provide excellent formative assessments and can easily be reviewed to name what students can do and cannot yet do, as well as how they are progressing in visible ways. Of course, once visual strategies evolve into final projects and presentations, then students need to be involved in articulating and applying rigorous critical standards for their work, on the basis of procedural understandings that are displayed, deep conceptual knowledge that is demonstrated, and the quality of the represented product.

READING IS SEEING
Why Teaching Students to Visualize Is So Important

Close your eyes. Think of a favorite novel—perhaps one from your youth or a current favorite. Recover a favorite scene. For example, I can picture a Hardy Boys mystery: Frank, Joe, and their pudgy friend Chet, who's wearing a red flannel shirt and jeans, bushwhacking through the woods in the moonlight. Chet is sweating and breathing hard and muttering "Gee whiz!" whenever a branch slaps him in the face. I next see them untethering a boat and motoring slowly across the wind-whipped ocean waves out to the old lighthouse, dark clouds scudding across the moon.

Scenes from our reading can be emblazoned in our memories for a lifetime. These images are a significant part of what makes reading intense, engaging, enjoyable, accessible, and usable—both at the moment of reading and afterwards. Images and the ideas connected to them become a part of us, and we call them forth as tools to help us think about issues or events in our current lives.

Based on my research on engaged reading, I've argued that being able to create images, story worlds, and mental models while one reads is an essential element of reading comprehension, engagement, and reflection (Wilhelm, 1997/2008). In fact, without visualization, students cannot comprehend, and readers cannot be said to be reading.

What Are Visualization Strategies: A Quick Sketch of Them in Action

In later chapters, I'll share various strategies and projects in detail, but so you have a good picture of them right away, here's a glimpse of how a bunch of boys I taught in Wisconsin used visualization strategies. I'll spotlight a boy named Scott, who probably had the most to gain from the strategies.

Scott was a student who had been mainstreamed into my EEN (exceptional education needs) seventh-grade reading/language arts program. He was labeled LD and ED and had failed reading the year before, and his sixth-grade teacher had told me that he didn't think Scott could really read. It was clear that Scott was a poor reader who had had several special education labels attached to him during his school history.

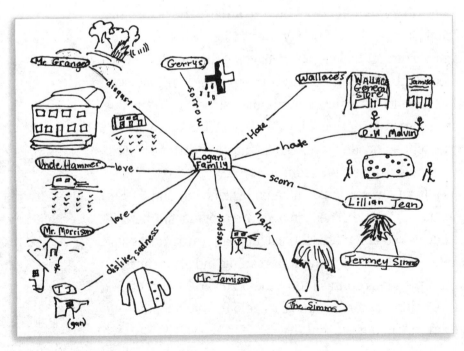

A picture map of *Roll of Thunder, Hear My Cry.* A student's complex thinking about relationships in the story is distilled into a few words and pictures.

And he was dragging those labels around, clunking them against each other and himself, like they were the chain carried by Marley's ghost.

Through informal chats with Scott, I found that he had many interests and that he passionately wanted to be a better reader (mostly so he could read to pursue his interests). He was very frustrated with school, which caused him to act out often; he would sometimes lie on the classroom floor in a near catatonic state of frustration. He said, "School makes me look stupid. Isn't school supposed to make you smart? Nobody helps me to read. Teachers just tell me I'm a bad reader and that I'm always wrong, but nobody helps me." Scott's poor reading clearly caused him many social frustrations as well as academic ones.

When I asked him what he saw when he read, he griped, "I can't see anything. I don't see anything when I read."

I made a deal with Scott. We'd spend lunch periods reading comic books, graphic novels, and picture books on topics related to our classroom work, an idea inspired by Margaret Meek's work with illiterate boys (Meek, et al., 1983). We'd try some visual techniques to help his comprehension. In return, he would try his best and also try to keep his nose clean and out of trouble—as much as was humanly possible!

It was a challenge, but Scott and I both stuck with it. There were some rough patches, but Scott began to slowly, ever so slowly, grow as a reader and become a part of our classroom learning projects.

Later in the school year, I walked into my classroom to find my seventh-grade class abuzz. It was the end of our civil rights unit. We'd been pursuing the question: "What are civil rights, and how can we protect them?" We'd done some reading and activities in common, but now students had teamed up to pursue their own research. Groups of four or five students were working in tight clusters of desks creating picture maps of the major ideas they'd learned so far about their various inquiry questions. Scott was working in a group of five boys who were sprawled on beanbag chairs.

Two were kids I considered good readers, two were fairly average, and one was Scott. United by their love of baseball, they were inquiring into the experience of black baseball players who played in the Negro Leagues and then helped to break the color line in the major leagues. They wanted to know what it took to successfully break this barrier. They had been focusing on the personal character of players like Jackie Robinson, but their reading had now prompted them to consider other factors as well.

Scott was presenting six big pictures he had created on sheets of chart paper. These were main-idea tableaux, and they visually summarized what he considered to be the main ideas

Consider This

In inquiry frameworks for curriculum, students can progress from their own current abilities and interests, do different kinds of work, and still contribute to the common learning project of the classroom. Since students negotiate their own research questions and readings around the central topic, teaching can be naturally differentiated, and individual needs accommodated.

Consider This

of *Teammates*, a picture book by Peter Goldenbock about the friendship between Brooklyn Dodgers players Pee Wee Reese and Jackie Robinson. Under my guidance, Scott had been reading a lot of picture books and easy readers that were appropriate to his ability, and he was learning a lot about his group's topic. He was also making valuable contributions to the group's project, which was to create a video documentary addressing their question. I couldn't help but notice that Scott looked happy, engaged, and involved with his classmates, and that they in turn were listening closely to him and taking him seriously.

Five of Scott's six pictures depicted Jackie Robinson with supportive characters from his life: Negro League players, fans, Branch Rickey (the general manager who invited Jackie to join the Brooklyn Dodgers), and Pee Wee Reese (the white all-star player who did so much to help Jackie overcome the prejudice he faced). Only one of the pictures showed the fans and teammates who resisted Jackie's place on the Dodgers' baseball team. This surprised Scott: "When I was drawing main ideas, I was surprised that most of them were helping instead of hurting pictures. That made me really think."

Scott told his group, "Drawing these made me see how important other people were [to Jackie's successfully breaking the color barrier]. We're right that Jackie put up with lots of prejudice and had to be brave, play good, and not fight back and all that, but he also needed these other people, or he wouldn't have been able to do it. I think we have to include this as part of our answer."

As Scott talked, Robin was busily adding the categories "black leaders," "black teammates," "fans," "white leaders," and "white teammates" to the semantic-feature analysis the group had been making to keep track of what helped or hindered various players, such as Jackie Robinson and Hank Aaron, in their efforts to be successful in the major leagues.

Steven jotted notes. "We definitely have to show two of Scott's scenes in our video," he chimed. "The one with Branch Rickey and one where Pee Wee puts his arm around Jackie in Cincinnati." As the other boys nodded, he started to sketch out a storyboard that would fit these scenes into their developing documentary.

Throughout their project, the boys used visualization strategies for various purposes:

- Scott used the tableaux (something we had worked on during our lunches together) to help himself comprehend his reading: to visualize scenes, identify main ideas, generate new ideas, and place-hold these for sharing with his group members.

- Robin contributed to the group's semantic-feature analysis, a guide to seeing patterns across the various texts group members had read.

- Steven sketched a storyboard that provided a format for sequencing and representing various ideas for their video documentary, a visual project that engaged the boys and focused their discussion and learning.

Two Key Research-Proven Highlights

Visualization improves key comprehension skills: Imagery and visualization treatments have achieved demonstrable success in various kinds of studies of the most intractable instructional problems around improving reading. For example, visualization has been successful in improving comprehension monitoring, a skill integral to expert reading, identifying main ideas from extended texts and justifying these with evidence from across that text, and seeing patterns of details across a text or texts to discover and justify complex implied relationships and how they work to create meaning (an essential tool for thinking and learning in any discipline). These are skills that are necessary to meeting the CCSS. According to the National Assessments of Educational Progress, fewer than six percent of our high school seniors can effectively use these procedures and score at the advanced levels of proficiency (see Jerry & Lutkus, NAEP, 2003; nationsreportcard.gov/reading_2009).

Visualization improves test scores in reading: Even cursory use of instruction supporting visualization improves scores on standardized tests. Personally, I do not hold stock in standardized test scores. I am convinced that such tests miss what is most important about reading and writing achievement and at the same time serve to dumb down both teaching and learning (see *The Testing Trap*, Hillocks, 2001, for a powerful study demonstrating how this is so; see also Shepard, 2000, for an excellent description of how such tests fail to accommodate what we know about human motivation and learning). Nonetheless, I work in schools and understand the political realities of test scores. Some ingenious studies (see Rose et al., 2000, and the Arts Education Partnership Critical Links study, 2002, www.aep-arts.org) have shown that imagery use has many benefits, including higher standardized reading scores relative to control groups.

Throughout, the visuals helped the boys to read, respond, analyze, organize, and represent their learning. These tools leveled the playing field, allowing weaker readers to elbow into the contest by making accessible the strategies of expert players of the reading game, and by extending the abilities of the accomplished readers.

The Social Advantage

In addition to the research-based benefits of visualization strategies, there are some other documented and common sense ones I'd like to highlight. First, students read visual texts in many arenas: cartoons, television shows and movies, websites, and other multimedia texts, video games, and much more. So it makes sense to use visuals in the classroom and to build on these other cultural literacies as we promote more academic literacies. After all, the only resource we have to teach students something new is what they already know and are interested in. Indeed, we must value and use these cultural resources—and students' facility with them—to reach and teach them as readers and composers. Let them use their current "funds of knowledge" to address and develop new strengths.

Second, inviting children to create visual responses to texts is an effective bridge to other composing literacies, such as writing and multimedia design.

Third, by embracing a wide variety of literacies in the classroom, you invite opportunities for students to interact and collaborate that often don't occur in traditional reading and writing instructional settings. Let's face it, we all like company, and students in upper elementary and middle school may be at the height of this need to socialize. Visualization projects are wonderfully interactive.

And last, when students compose and explore ideas together through various literacies, such as murals, newspapers, websites, and videos, they gain access to democratic avenues of meaning making. After all, "communities of practice" in the real world use multiple literacies to solve problems and negotiate meanings—why shouldn't our students? In offering them many viable literacies, we apprentice them for real-world activities where they will be required to demonstrate their understanding in many ways, including making visual products.

Despite these many research-proven benefits for both struggling and accomplished readers, a review of instructional materials and textbooks reveals that visual strategies are rarely presented. This leaves it to us, the teachers, to provide students with visual strategies that are appropriate to their needs as readers.

It's hard to explain why visual strategies are not more widely used, except that perhaps they don't match up with what Ken Zeichner calls "the salience of the traditional"—the traditional notions of how to teach and "do" school. This is something we will all have to work to consciously overcome for the benefit of our students, particularly now, because we cannot meet the challenges of our current moment nor the appropriate goals set down by the Common Core State Standards, unless we find a new way of teaching that is more in line with what we know about human motivation and learning from a robust research base in social psychology and cognitive science. Understanding and meeting this challenge, writ large, is the subject of the next chapter.

A student expresses her understanding of the changing states of matter through a cartoon. As teachers, we need to involve kids in many types of literate expression.

CHAPTER 3

WHAT DOES IT MEAN TO TEACH?

Grounding Our Instruction in Current Research and Theory

A s my mother used to say: "Out of the mouths of babes . . . can come great wisdom." I've learned from thirty years of working with kids that if you listen hard enough, you can gain great insight. Sometimes, students are more hip to current learning theory and research than their teachers! This was certainly the case with Curtis. When Curtis stopped by to see me during that lunch and lamented that school "isn't about the kids any more," I read him a poem to lift his spirits, a poem about a subject I knew he knew well: hunting. That this poem about a father teaching his son would move him to say, "People in real life teach each other that way, but teachers never do" and thereby lay out a challenge for all teachers in our school— *that* I didn't predict. But I was grateful for his honest response because it gave me a window into his needs. It also indicated that he knew what cognitive scientists have been showing us for years: that teaching is assistance in actual contexts of use, provided at the point of need, to help us to do things we cannot yet do alone.

Curtis went on to tell me that he was having trouble in math because he couldn't understand word problems. I said I would try to help him. Now, I had several choices. I could have lectured Curtis on the mathematical principles he needed. I could have shown him correctly solved word problems, hoping he'd be able to tease out the thinking processes involved, but that seemed a bit like trying to teach someone to play the saxophone by having them listen to John Coltrane CDs. Or I could have just urged Curtis to keep fiddling around with the assigned word problems until he "discovered" how to do them.

I chose another course, albeit a rare one in American schools. We went through the math book and found some word problems about maple sugaring, since he had done some sugaring on his uncle's farm. I then "thought aloud" about how I would do one of these problems in three steps. I drew pictures of the process and created a chart that showed the available data and the data that was missing. After my think-aloud, Curtis and I identified all the strategies I used. We discussed other ways of solving the problem and the advantages and pitfalls of each. Then I did another problem and asked Curtis to help me at various points. After a few more problems, Curtis took the lead and I helped him (if other students had been around, I would have had them help each other), and by the end of the period, Curtis completed a word problem on his own.

Curtis departed a few minutes before the bell, saying, "I think I've kind of got it now." Off he went, exiting my room and heading out into the stream of humanity heading up from the lunchroom. Spinning a paper clip in my hand, I thought about Curtis, who would be out on his own in the world one day. I hoped I had used a process of assistance that would let him do some of the work of mathematicians wherever in life this kind of thinking would be required of him.

In the past I might have just told Curtis what to do or to figure it out on his own. But studying, reflecting on my own learning, and considering how various methods of teaching helped struggling readers led me to the learning-centered style of teaching I used with Curtis. This didn't happen overnight. My journey to learning-centered teaching was filled with many challenges and not a few missteps.

Teaching as a Theoretical Battleground

Now I'll lay my cards on the table. In this chapter, I'm going to try to lead you to see why learning-centered teaching is the superior stance to take; the only one that teaches for transfer, understanding, and use; and the only one that will help our students to meet the CCSS. Even if I don't convince you, you'll walk away at chapter's end with the research-based theoretical backdrop for the teaching ideas in this book. I will put in boldface the points I'd like you to carry away and "tattoo on your forehead" (as I put it to the preservice teachers I coach).

All teaching is theoretical.

Many teachers I've talked with profess to have little patience with theory. They argue that they are on the front lines, dealing with individual students' needs each day, so they don't have time for "pie in the sky" stuff. In fact, every dealing we undertake and every decision we make is theoretical. We do what we do and decide what we decide because of beliefs that this teaching "move" will work in this situation with this child or this group. Being unaware of our theories means we cannot test them—consider how happy we are with them—which keeps us from improving and using theoretical principles in ways that would benefit our own teaching and our students' learning. This keeps us from achieving the reflective practice of a professional teacher.

Everything we do in a classroom expresses a theory of learning.

When I walk into a classroom and see a lectern in the front and all the desks in rows, I see a theory expressed. What is revealed is a teacher-centered content-oriented view of information transmission: that the teacher has the information students need and will purvey it to them through talk. If the classroom has learning centers and small clusters of desks, an entirely different theory is expressed: a student-centered or learning-centered outlook that believes students will learn best by engaging in projects that they work on together, with the help of the teacher.

Understanding theory makes our teaching more powerful.

Understanding the theoretical foundations of the ideas in this book will help you use teaching and reading strategies to much greater effect. Instead of getting a grab bag of ideas, I want you to have a powerful lens for thinking about teaching and learning—and teaching reading and composing in particular. I want you to take away articulate principles of teaching and learning that you can use to think with across teaching cases. Understanding the theoretical underpinnings will allow you to adapt all of the ideas here to your needs, and to invent new ones, depending on the needs and situations of your students.

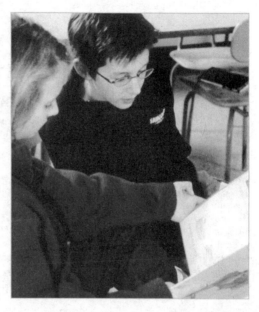

The Learning-Centered Model

Rogoff proposes that research in cognitive science over the past 30 years demonstrates that we need a "multi-sided" model that accommodates the *what*, the *who* of the learner, the multiple *whos* of disciplinary experts, and most importantly,

Every teacher must ask questions like "How can I best teach my students to read?"

the *why* and the *how* of learning as well as the *when* and *where* of the context in which learning takes place and is used. This model focuses on the relationship between the teacher and learner, the text and the reader, and on the relationship between the knowledge (emphasizing strategic processes to be learned, just like the CCSS) and the contexts, or "community of practice," in which such knowledge is learned and will be used. Rogoff calls this approach the "learning-centered" model, though it is alternatively known as the sociocultural, Vygotskian, teaching/learning-centered, and co-constructivist model. The purpose of this model is to "transform the participation" of learners from that of novices into that of more expert practitioners who are actually involved in whatever field of endeavor is associated with the knowledge domain under study.

As an example, take the case of making spaghetti sauce. The information-centered theory would provide recipes to students. The student-centered theory would ask students to "discover" their own recipes. But in learning-centered theory students would be apprenticed and inducted into cultural knowledge about making spaghetti sauce, the chemistry of cuisine, the elements and spices to use; as one learns, one can begin to adapt this knowledge and extend it in personal ways. You must be apprenticed into the cultural knowledge of making Ragu.

Interestingly, Miles Myers, the former executive director of the National Council of Teachers of English (NCTE), argues forcefully in his book *Changing Our Minds* (1996) that the literacy taught in school is always 30 years or more behind the literacy demands and uses of current society. In other words, teaching is regarded

With the learning-centered approach the interactions between teachers and students in the context of meaningful situations are crucial.

as donating established sets of information to students rather than inviting them to work side-by-side with respected mentors inside "communities of practice" where students experience reading and writing in the service of accomplishing real goals in the real world. Likewise, the cognitive researcher Rich Lehrer from Vanderbilt's Cognition and Technology Group makes the point, in a personal communication, that teaching in schools is almost always 30 to 50 years behind the research understandings in cognition and learning.

Learning-Centered: Some Key Ideas

- Orientation is interactive/transactional—learning must attend to student interests, current knowledge, goals, and the cultural knowledge to be learned from using the text.

- Theories of socio-culturalism and co-constructivism support this model.

- Focus is on the *why* and the *how*—the purposes, contexts, and relationships in which the procedures of knowledge production and performance are learned.

- Teaching is assisting learners to do what they cannot yet do on their own, in the context of real situations in which the learning is necessary and useful.

- Learning is not natural but cultural—knowledge is socially and culturally constructed, so learning is a result of the opportunities and assistance provided by more knowledgeable practitioners of the studied material and processes.

- Reading is constructing understanding through conversing and transacting with a text, attending to the cultural codes it expresses and the way it has been constructed.

- Reading requires using one's life experiences and attending to the cultural conventions and meanings that a text uses to communicate.

- Meaning is in the conversation between the reader and the text, where the reader's needs and interests meet the communicated meanings of the text.

- Comprehension is the ability to construct a meaningful personal response that is respectful of and attends to the text's communicated meaning.

- Authorial and Transactional Reader-Response theories of literary experience and interpretation are consistent with this model.

- Valid interpretation accounts for the reader's needs and the coded meanings of the text.

- To teach reading, provide assistance to students who are reading challenging texts to undertake real-world projects or address real-world issues. Becoming a better reader requires help using new strategies and understanding sophisticated textual conventions in meaningful contexts—analogous to those in which literacy is used in the real world.

Text Complexity Standards

The new Common Core standards are clearly in line with learning-centered teaching, and the standards themselves can only be met—both literally and in spirit—through rigorous inquiry approaches to learning. I cannot possibly convey how passionately I believe in this approach. My professional life is inhabited by students who suffer intensely in school, never seeing the payoff of true learning. Like Curtis, many poignantly understand that school fails to meet their human needs, and fails utterly to teach them in any personally meaningful or functional way. The fact that there is a powerful alternative endorsed by more than 30 years of research in literacy and cognitive science that is rarely used drives me to distraction. It's as if doctors were still bleeding patients with leeches long after it had been established that such a practice was not only unhelpful but deleterious. Yet I have great hopes for the future, especially in light of the new Common Core, which provides us with a visionary and historic opportunity to change teaching and learning for the benefit of all. (For a thorough review of different theories of learning and reading, and their instructional implications, see Wilhelm, Baker, & Dube, 2001.)

The Learning-Centered Model: Important Tenets

Below are a few of the important features of the learning-centered model.

All learning is social and transactional.

A student, or indeed any learner, learns by transacting with another consciousness (through direct interaction or through a text, such as a book or website).

Bruner (1986), using Vygotsky, argues that the driving force behind all learning is social interaction in the context of "joint productive activity" (completing a significant task with the help of others more expert) as opposed to being told something (curriculum-centered/information-transmission) or being encouraged to do something on one's own (student-centered).

Learning is an apprenticeship to a community of practice.

Learning transactions are an entry into particular cultures or communities of practice that make, use, and perform knowledge. This might mean entry into a content domain, such as science, a trade, such as carpentry, or a group of readers, such as science-fiction or fantasy aficionados. To be inducted into the culture, you must be taught the language, strategies, goals, and other cultural knowledge by expert practitioners in that culture because the knowledge does not exist apart from that culture. For example, you are in a restaurant and order a bacon, lettuce, and tomato sandwich on lightly toasted rye bread and a Beefeater martini straight up with a twist. The waiter writes Bf (m)/↑(tw), slaps the slip on the cocktail counter, and then yells through the grill window: "BLT on whiskey down!" Learning to be a waiter means learning certain procedures, terms, and codes. Listen to bridge players or golfers discuss their games, and it will be just as rich. In short, these groups use lingo with a lot of specialized knowledge behind it

Knowing how to do something means being fluent in the language and strategies of that performance.

When I learned to whitewater kayak, I had to learn not only the skills of Eskimo rolling, "peeling out" into heavy current, and "eddying in" to calm water, but also this vocabulary and how to use it to "see" the river—plan and execute "catches" of "micro-eddies" (small quiet pools of water in whitewater from which one can "scout" or rest), plan "lines" (routes) through rocky descents, and use "sweeps," "boofs," and other moves to execute these "lines." Learning these strategies and terms was part of the entry into the cultural knowledge of the kayaking fraternity; it was how I became a full-fledged member of this "culture" or community of practice.

What is learned must be taught.

A tenet of Vygotskian theory is that what is learned must be taught, precisely because it is cultural and conventional—it is not natural, like, say, learning to walk. Particular groups of people have created the knowledge, invented the terminology, and devised the appropriate procedures as they practiced certain kinds of activities together. To join, you must be taught their forms of special knowledge. Visual tools are an excellent way of doing this, since they make sophisticated, abstract strategies and content visible and available to learners.

Learners move on a continuum from novice practice to more expert practice.

So how do we give children the lingo and moves they need to get into the expert reading club? This is where Vygotsky's concept of the zone of proximal development (ZPD) is useful. Vygotsky defines the ZPD as "the distance between the actual developmental level (of the learner) as determined by independent problem-solving and the level of potential development as determined through problem-solving under adult guidance or in collaboration with more capable peers" (Vygotsky, 1978). In other words, what students can already do we should allow them to do on their own. (This is a student's "independent learning" level.) What they cannot do on their own but can do with our help (called the "instructional level") should be the substance of what we teach them.

I am a learning-centered teacher. The apprenticeship model makes the most sense to me as a parent, a teacher, and a researcher.

Teaching is providing assistance to the child to do what she cannot yet do on her own.

The assistance we provide students to help and support them to be successful in meeting new challenges (which they could not meet on their own) is the stuff of teaching. In this book, visualization strategies comprise the powerful teaching support that assists students through their ZPD.

Good teaching is always in the learner's zone of proximal development.

Students asked to work only at their independent level do what they can already do and learn nothing new. What students cannot do successfully even with assistance is something they should not be asked to do (such tasks are at their "frustrational level"). Students who cannot be successful with a task even if we help them end up learning worse than nothing—they learn that reading is too hard or stupid or that they are not readers. Useful teaching proceeds in the ZPD, the student's instructional learning level.

Different students have different ZPDs, so instructional methods must be flexible.

A significant challenge to teachers is that all students in a classroom have somewhat different zones of proximal development. This means that we have to teach them in ways that assist them through those zones to higher levels of actual development. Visualization strategies are great for this because they are so flexible. They can be used to help both struggling readers and more advanced readers to improve from their own level and become more competent readers using particular strategies, such as reading for main ideas. Visual techniques are ways to meet all learners in their ZPD and assist them at their current level of reading accomplishment. Likewise, learning-centered inquiry environments allow students to read different texts that are appropriate for them and to be taught in slightly different ways, while still engaging in a common classroom project.

We bring
all we've
experienced
in life to each
and every
text we read.

Building From the Known to the New

Okay, so teaching and learning are social and relational, what we learn is cultural and is used to solve problems, and the ZPD is the window for new learning. There is one more central sociocultural insight for you to put in your pocket: To learn something new, we have to use our current resources and connect what is already known to the new.

In cognitive research, this has long been known as a basic tenet of schema theory. A schema is an organized set of all knowledge you possess about a particular topic or issue. This knowledge is systematic and patterned and usually includes a repertoire of strategies to help solve problems. Learning requires that existing schema be used and then either added to (accommodated) or revised and restructured (adapted) in the face of the new learning.

When expert readers read, they immediately access schematic knowledge to visualize and build meaning. What background do you access when you read the following statement? "Blinds for sale." What do you think it is about?

This statement usually causes readers to begin imagining venetian blinds and window treatments and to activate schema about redecorating their home. When the second statement—"Goose hunting season opens soon"—is revealed, the reader must recognize that she activated the incorrect schema. It is interesting that in Wisconsin and Maine—where bird hunting is common—many people do initially activate the hunting schema because this is "close to home." In other parts of the country, this rarely happens. This demonstrates how we naturally apply and build meaning from our past experience. Now try this one: "She ran quickly toward the rising sun…"

This statement often stimulates readers to begin visualizing a female jogger doing her morning workout or a girl running down the beach toward her lover. When they read "…knowing fresh oats would be in the barn," they must recognize they are in the wrong schema and self-correct—they must bring a new set of schematic knowledge of horses and barnyards to bear as they revise what they envision. If they do not have any experience with or schema knowledge of farms, then they will not be able to envision this revised meaning. One boy in this situation told me in response, "They must be serving oatmeal in the barn." He did not have the requisite schema to correctly envision the sentence. Another said: "It must be a cow," and the farm kids laughed. Why? They knew cows are ungulates and eat grasses, not oats. This is how much authors depend on their readers' pr-existing schema.

So where is the meaning when we read? Is it totally in the text? If this were the case, all readers would discern the same meaning, but as we see above, they do not. Is the meaning totally in the reader's head? If this were the case, we could not say that my student was wrong about a jogger eating Quaker oatmeal in the barn after her run, or that the runner is a cow. Or is meaning created somewhere between the reader's knowledge and needs and the verbally coded information offered by the text? It is obvious to me, from examples such as these and from my research with adolescent

The Zone of Proximal Development (ZPD)

Students all possess a current zone of actual development (ZAD)—their current independent abilities. The zone of proximal development ZPD defines the lower and upper limits of successful instruction. If teaching is pitched too high and students cannot be successful even with help, then students will become frustrated and not learn. If it is too low, then students simply repeat what they already know—or they get bored and distracted.

The ZPD for any student is not a "fixed attribute" but is co-constructed through teacher-student relationships around particular tasks (Wells, 1999). In other words, the ZPD is constantly unfolding and is more an attribute of the situation in which one learns (e.g., by interacting with experts around real tasks) than an attribute of individuals.

readers, that reading is a transaction that requires a conversation between a reader, her schema, and the codes and conventions of the text.

Consider this example:

> I walk around the house all day
> Run through the yard
> And help with play
> When nighttime falls I find my place and
> Underneath the bed I'll stay.

In this case, the reader needs not only to activate conceptual/topical schematic knowledge (of shoes) but schematic knowledge of genre (the text type riddle) and procedures (appropriate strategies—seeing complex implied relationships and making self-to-text connections). Recognizing the text as a riddle helps us to activate the proper interpretive operations. We have to recognize the tip-off for the game we are in, and we have to know the rules of the game: We must see the common thread across deliberately mysterious cues to identify what is being described. If we don't know that this is what riddles ask us to do, we'll have to build our schema by being taught these rules and strategic moves before we can be successful with this text and others that are like it.

Recognizing that this poem is a riddle means that we know we must solve the riddle. It also means we must know to do so by matching the description provided metaphorically (through personification) with an inanimate object that is quite tangentially described and is unnamed.

If students possess the conceptual/topical, genre/text type, and procedural/strategic knowledge they need, then we need to help them activate this background. We need to help them to notice the conventional tip-offs that tell them they must activate such knowledge. For example, with the riddle they must recognize that they are being asked to complete the metaphor and then "fill in the blank" of the comparison. If they do not possess the requisite schematic knowledge, we must teach them this knowledge before they begin to read a text that requires it. Only learning-centered theories fully recognize—and emphasize—that students need to be helped to know how to read new kinds of texts (e.g., fables, extended definitions, classifications, ironic monologues) as well as textual conventions (e.g., the codes of irony or symbolism). In teacher-centered approaches, students are taught by being lectured, assigned tasks, and evaluated on their performance; in student-centered ones, by engaging with self-chosen texts on their own.

Schema: Unique as a Fingerprint

As Gambrell and Koskinen (2002) point out in their excellent review, it is important for the teacher to understand that students' spontaneous use of imagery will be individual and unique, shaped by their personal experiences and background knowledge. If you ask students to imagine a wristwatch, for instance, some may imagine an analog watch with hands, others a digital watch with flashing numbers, some a Mickey Mouse watch, and still others a Swatch. Some young people, who tell time with a cell phone, may imagine an older person wearing this "single function device!" There is a direct relationship between a student's experiential background and both comprehension and imagery, since students must draw on their experience to comprehend and create images. If students do not have those resources, they must be provided the requisite experiences—with photographs, movies, objects, labs, drama work, field trips, and so on before they read.

Teachers and students both need to understand that while there are no absolutely right or wrong ways of imagining a text, and that their images will be unique and idiosyncratic, there are valid and invalid images. The best and most valid images are those that combine personal background experience with direct and implied cues from a text to create a visualization that is consistent with and respectful of all the details of a text's coded construction. These are the kinds of images that best promote textual comprehension.

Good Teaching Is Sequenced

Text Complexity Standards

No matter what the content we're teaching, we need to sequence our teaching so that it starts where students currently are and guides them to where they need to be. (This will be the only possible way to meet the CCSS standards for text complexity.) This book will explore how to use visualization strategies in such sequences. The following model demonstrates what I mean by a sequential process of teaching.

Q&A 2: Describe the three-step teaching approach you advocate for in this book. Why is this effective?

Pre-Assess: Identify Students' Needs
The teacher ascertains which strategies students need but don't yet know how to use. This can be done through pre-assessments using think-alouds, action strategies, visuals, and so forth.

2 Modeling: I Do/You Watch

The teacher models the use of a challenging new strategy in the context where it is needed, and the students watch.

3 Sharing Expertise: I Do/You Help

The teacher uses the strategy, citing the tip-off in the text that signals the need, and activates the required interpretive operations. She asks the students to help out by citing subsequent tip-offs and talking the teacher's way through the strategy.

4 Gradual Release: You Do Together/I Help

Students work together in small groups to find the tip-offs and practice using the required strategy.

5 Assessing Mastery: You Do/I Watch

Finally, individual students use the strategy independently. If they cannot, they continue working in groups or with the help of the teacher. The important thing is for the student to get the right amount of support to be successful—to move through the ZPD (to a new ZAD).

These are the steps I used with Curtis and the process that I propose that you use with all students. It comprises a form of what is known as scaffolding— providing very explicit and active assistance in handing over expert knowledge that helps students to master new strategies. I use several elaborated versions of this model throughout this book.

Scaffolding for a particular strategy can be applied in different ways to meet the different needs of various students in your classroom. For example, I might continue working with small groups of struggling students as they watch me use the strategy and then try to help me use it. Students who are getting it but still need some help work together. I'll drop in when I can to help. And those who can use the strategy independently can work at applying it on their own, or perhaps I'll find a more complicated textual challenge for using the strategy that they can address in small groups or on their own. In this way, everybody gets pushed and scaffolded appropriately to grow as far as they can.

Scaffolding itself is a very powerful metaphor for good teaching, so powerful I would like to pay some attention to this metaphor and the research around it. Wood, Bruner, & Ross (1976) were the first researchers to use this metaphor as they described how mothers guide their young children to develop language. These researchers demonstrated that parents who were successful scaffolders:

- took advantage of real situations in which language could be developed and applied with real consequences—they taught in real contexts at the point of need.

- considered the child's interests, goals, and current abilities.

- focused the child's attention on the task at hand.

- kept them motivated to work on the task.

- modeled successful completion of the task, as often as necessary for the child to internalize the strategies.

- encouraged the child to participate in helping them complete the task, if the child could not do it alone.

- divided tasks into manageable chunks, so that success was attainable.

- kept the task at the appropriate level of difficulty (in the child's zone of proximal development).

- lent help and expertise at the point of need when necessary for the child to successfully complete the task.

- offered a variety of support "customized" to the current needs of the child in the current situation—they used not just one boilerplate method but constantly experimented and varied their approach.

- used feedback from observing the child to inform subsequent instruction— their teaching was responsive and reciprocal, and the child provided feedback about what worked and didn't work and therefore how she needed to be taught.

- introduced new tasks to provide a constant state of challenge, continually "upping the ante" by asking for more sophisticated responses ("fah" might be accepted for *fish*, then "fishy," but children were never allowed to backslide and were continually challenged to be more specific, expert, and precise).

- directed attention to relevant features of the task and developed situationally based strategies for dealing with these features.

- asked the child to complete the task on her own, but only when this could be done with a probability of success.

The goal of such scaffolding is for the learner to internalize mental functions, such as mastering spoken language or reading strategies, so that these can be independently used. But achieving this goal requires sensitive, persistent, and relational teaching. It is not easy work. The standard placed on the accomplished teacher for providing scaffolding is a high one.

Purposeful Learning and Reading: Macro and Micro Purposes

The last point I want to make in this chapter is that scaffolding must serve both macro and micro purposes. In other words, whatever we teach has to resonate inside the classroom and at the present moment *and* outside the classroom now and in the foreseen future. And we have to let our students know that it will—that whatever it is they are sweating over is useful knowledge they can transfer to their lives outside of school. That it is functional and does and will count! The issue of transfer is central to education: if we do not teach students something during a class that they can then use in their next class or in their lives, then we have taught them nothing.

Why raise the bar so high? Because while teacher-centered theories are oriented toward the past, and established sets of information, and student-centered theories are focused on the present, on what the student is interested in and can do now, learning-centered teaching and scaffolding are future-oriented. They are focused on what the student can do next. It is an instructional style that seeks to build specific strategies and capacities among groups of students and among individuals. Because of this future orientation, scaffolding requires clear goals, a clear focus on actual tasks, and lots of assistance to help students make each new leap into the possibilities of the future.

Defining Our Goals

I've argued that inquiry is the most powerful way to conceive of curriculum and teaching (see Hillocks, 1995, 1999; Wilhelm, 1997/2008; Wilhelm & Friedemann, 1998; Wilhelm & Edmiston, 1998; Smith & Wilhelm, 2002, Beach & Myers, 2002; Wilhelm, 2007; Wilhelm & Novak, 2011 for data-driven arguments for this position). In fact, I've argued that reading and writing are best thought of as forms of inquiry and best taught in the context of inquiry (see especially Wilhelm, 2007).

We've seen that every content area is a community of practice. This community can be considered a field of inquiry that produces and uses knowledge. Knowing what strategies expert practitioners in science or math make use of can help us to

Every activity we give our students should serve an overarching goal. I want my students to be skilled enough to exercise choices in their lives and flexibly apply strategies to new situations.

Focus on College, Career, and Citizenship Readiness

apprentice our "novice experts," so that they can read and think with the same kind of intellectual tools.

Once we understand the kinds of seminal tasks to be engaged, we can identify the strategic demands of these tasks and consider how to build an instructional sequence—or a scaffold of activities—that will help students to develop the necessary skills over time, text by text and activity by activity, as they climb the ladder towards expertise. To do this, we need specific teaching goals.

First, I need macro goals, or global goals. My own macro goal is to help my students become independent readers, writers, problem solvers, and learners, so that they can exercise choices in their lives and serve community interests by being active, democratic citizens. My awareness of this goal helps me ask how what I am doing each day serves this global end. If my instruction does not serve this end, I can ask how it can be amended to better do so. What issues are my students and I inquiring into? What knowledge and functions do I hope they will master and apply? What is the ultimate "end" of my teaching?

Likewise, I need micro goals and micro scaffolds at the local level of daily instruction and minute-by-minute interactions with particular kids. How is my lesson-by-lesson work serving my global ends and the ultimate goals of our inquiry or unit? I need to understand the task at hand, and how the assistance I provide will help students to develop strategies for meeting the goals and completing the tasks.

Scaffolding in Action: Skating With My Friend Gary

My friend Gary Feight is a consummate teacher. One of his favorite things to teach is ice hockey skating. I've often seen him take a child struggling to skate and transform him or her into an incredibly powerful skater. I've watched him teach several times under the glaring halogen lights above the glaze of ice at the West Bend hockey rink. And I've seen him use scaffolding intelligently when he teaches.

The first comment Gary makes to a new student is, "I've got to learn you before I can teach you." So he gets to know his new charges, discovering their motivations for learning to skate and the state of their current abilities. After chatting for a while, he'll ask his student to take some turns around the rink, saying, "You skate and I'll follow." Gary is typically attired in his brown canvas coat and a black wool hat that looks like a skullcap, since it appears to be a size too small. He'll skate behind his student and ask him to do some stops and other moves. He'll watch carefully and nod to himself, taking mental note of exactly what the student does and doesn't do. From this, Gary learns what the student can do (zone of actual development) and therefore what he can do next with his help (zone of proximal development).

Gary tells me, "You have to start by making kids feel good, by showing them they already have some skill and ability and therefore the potential for future success. Then you show them how you can build from their current competence to continued growth."

When Gary teaches a new move, he'll say, "I'll skate, you follow" (I do/you watch). Then he typically gives his students drills to practice the skills involved. Quite often he makes the moves as he tows them or guides them along (I do/you help or you do/ I help). His younger students love it when he goes full bore with them in tow to give them the feel of particular moves, then turns and abruptly stops, ice chips flying into the air. There's a lot of laughter and chatter during Gary's lessons. "How did that feel?" he asked one young boy after towing him around the rink twice. "Holy cow!" the boy replied. "Will I ever be able to skate that fast?" "Ha!" Gary laughed. "In a year you'll think that what we just did was in slow motion, like molasses in the freezer!" The boy shakes his head and smiles in disbelief.

After teaching a technique, Gary then has a student try it independently and in a real situation (you do/I watch), such as in a hockey scrimmage. Gary has shown me that teaching in such a relational and scaffolded manner ultimately leads to independence—to students literally "skating away" on their own.

This is what we want for our students as readers, and this is what we explore in the next chapter: using the concreteness of visualization to scaffold our students up, up, and away into more heightened forms of reading.

CHAPTER 4

VISUAL STRATEGIES: PART OF THE PROCESSES AND PRODUCTS OF INQUIRY

Inquiring Minds Know How to See and Model

Inquiry is the process through which all knowledge was and is created. Inquiry is a rigorous response to human concerns and problems. For example, healers developed and continue to develop processes of healing and medical knowledge in conjunction (as process and concept always develop together) by collecting data about human maladies and how to address these over the course of time. Historians developed and continue to develop historical knowledge and processes in tandem by considering issues of conjoint living and how to think about and resolve these issues over the course of time. Inquiry is not only how we create knowledge, but also how learners are best inducted and apprenticed into expert understanding, and how they come to understand deeply and apply what they have learned.

It's impossible to imagine a doctor, historian, mathematician, environmentalist, educator, or anyone else becoming expert in their field without knowing how to solve problems by inquiring and learning from the environments in which they work. As Vygotskians proclaim in regard to education: teachers must learn from their students how best to teach them.

It's equally difficult to imagine pursuing inquiry, or representing the findings of inquiry, without using visual tools. Here's a personal story. For the past several years, my wife Peggy has suffered from a rare and as yet undiagnosed blood disease. Believe me, I know from dealings with the world's top research doctors at the Mayo Clinic and the National Institutes of Health that a doctor uses X-rays, MRIs, and many other kinds of images, physical models of the body, photographs, graphs, charts, and data maps of various kinds to organize, analyze, synthesize, diagnose, represent, explain, theorize, and problem solve various conditions.

And I have to tell you: I am on my knees every night thanking the Animating Spirit of the Universe for doctors such as these—caring people, certainly, but even more important to me: inquiring individuals who know that new problems cannot be addressed algorithmically, but must be pursued heuristically (this distinction is explored further below). That is, when facing new or evolving problems, we must get outside the box, get beyond established ways of knowing, and develop new processes and new kinds of knowledge whenever faced with new emerging problems. If it were not for doctors who sought knowledge this way, Peggy would not be alive. New conditions would not be identified or understood. New controls and cures would not be developed. Knowledge would not expand. The path of inquiry is the path of knowledge and problem solving—and can even be the path to joy and wisdom (Wilhelm & Novak, 2011).

Likewise, we cannot prepare our students for the current and future challenges of their lives and the world unless we teach them to inquire, and vigorously assist them in learning how to learn. I would contend, in fact, that the only thing worth learning is inquiry—that is, the only thing worth learning is learning how to learn.

Algorithms and Heuristics

Topical inquiry certainly involves learning the algorithmic thinking of a discipline, but true critical inquiry—or knowledge use and knowledge making that goes beyond what is already known and established—also involves using the informing principles of algorithms in highly creative, adaptable, and transferable ways in the form of heuristics.

An algorithm is a proven and effective method for solving a circumscribed typical problem with a concrete protocol of preset rules. An algorithm is typically expressed as a finite list of explicit, well-defined instructions for calculation, data processing, or automated reasoning. Interestingly, in my own research on engagement (Wilhelm, 1997/2008; Smith & Wilhelm, 2002; 2006; Wilhelm & Novak, 2011) I have found that students dismiss algorithmic thinking as "being told what to think" or "playing guess what the teacher already knows" unless it is clearly in service of understanding disciplinary thinking in some way that leads to heuristic thinking and the actual application of such thinking to the solving of new and evolving problems in the world. Daniel Pink (20011) describes the same phenomenon regarding motivation in his book *drive!*

The word *heuristic* comes from the same root as the word *eureka!* and means to find, figure out, or discover. A "heuristic" therefore refers to experience-based

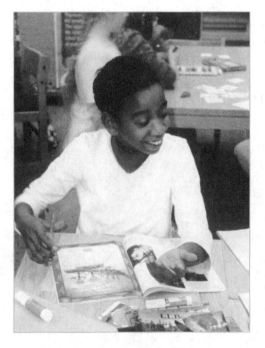

techniques based on general principles for solving a problem in a particular situation, for learning, or for discovery. In more precise terms, heuristics are problem-solving strategies using readily accessible and creatively applicable principles. A heuristic is a simple, flexible, and transportable thinking tool and can be conceptual or procedural. Some simple ones are to cover the five Ws + H in journalistic writing, to address the five kinds of knowledge whenever reading, composing, or working to understand (Wilhelm, Smith & Fredricksen, 2012), to accommodate the five themes of flow whenever creating environments to foster engagement and motivation (Smith & Wilhelm, 2002, 2006); to ask What do I want you to know/believe/do? (claim), what makes you say so? (data), so what? (warrant) when arguing since this is Toulmin's basic notion of argument (Smith & Wilhelm, 2006; Smith, Wilhelm & Fredricksen, 2012).

Heuristics differ from algorithms in that they are flexible repertoires and can be elaborated, tweaked, extended, complexified, and transformed in various ways to solve new problems in highly creative ways. Heuristics are web-like in that different kinds of knowledge and processes are set in creative relationship. Heuristics are often visual or involve visual elements. Algorithms are linear and pre-set.

When I teach in my Boise State Writing Project institutes, the teachers are asked to develop and present teaching demonstrations. These demonstrations are based on general principles that lead into heuristic thinking that is transferable across grade levels and cases. I always ask that the teachers present their thinking in multimodal ways and express their heuristics, or general rules of thumb, in multimodal ways. A teaching demonstration is immeasurably enhanced with videos of students, graphic displays or data, flow charts of the heuristic in action, and so on.

Visualizing as Inquiring

I am entirely convinced that inquiry is the most powerful way that we can possibly teach and the way in which students most naturally and deeply learn (see Wilhelm, 2007, and Wilhelm and Novak, 2011 for reviews of research supporting this contention). Inquiry is sometimes thought of as a loose kind of "noodling around" to discover and learn on one's own. But as a "term of art" in cognitive science, inquiry is anything but this. Inquiry is considered to be the rigorous apprenticeship into disciplinary ways of thinking, learning how to learn and create new knowledge with the methods of experts, and learning how to participate as knowledge makers in communities of practice.

There are various models of true inquiry, but all lead toward substantive disciplinary understandings and applications, and all are dialogic, collaborative, visual and "embodied"/experienced, sequenced, and involve joint productive meaning-making that apprentices learners, through "legitimate peripheral participation" (Lave & Wenger, 1991)—real activity that mirrors what real experts do—to ever more expert understanding and use. Visualization promotes and can constitute inquiry because it is active and embodied, is part of expert repertoire, involves application, and leads to future action. It connects the known to the new, and combines personal knowledge with the studied material and connects this back to the world.

Inquiry is likewise a form of "design": a way of negotiating, representing, and sharing carefully constructed meanings—including processes of understanding and problem solving. These representations involve visuals at various levels, including that of "mental modeling." Visuals can become a performance of understanding and a knowledge artifact, an intervention, a proposal, or solution to a problem, as well as a way to demonstrate literacy and problem-solving repertoires.

Erika Boas does wonderful work with historical inquiry in a unit framed by the question "What work do historians do?" She has students do a wide variety of visual work, starting with having students become historians, using digital cameras to collect data—taking pictures, videotaping interviews with informants, copying historical artifacts and documents, and so on. These can in turn be made into multimedia displays, interactive websites or kiosks, and museum exhibits archived on-line or for local history museums. At the end of the unit, students have not only created actual historical contributions, but have reflected deeply on what historians do. Erika also has students reflect on the processes they have learned through picture maps of the "thinking hats" of historians, brochures, and PSAs about what historians do and how they do it.

A well-documented problem with social science, mathematical, and science education is that students are taught these disciplines as a set of previously solved problems from a textbook. Students therefore have minimal opportunity to experience the open-ended inquiry into "ill-formed problems" that characterize the actual practice of any discipline. The Learning Through Collaborative Visualization (CoVis) project was an attempt to address this problem in science education by providing students with the ability to conduct their own inquiries using scientific visualization tools and to interact with scientists whose professional practice consists of exploring similar questions using similar tools. The project's work is archived at www.covis.northwestern.edu.

The bottom line? Inquiry promotes deep understanding, use, and transformed learning and being. Visualization is part and parcel of inquiry and understanding. As such, we must cultivate visualization strategies for our students as a way of comprehending and inquiring into the most compelling problems.

Student visual projects from a "What Makes Me Me?" inquiry unit about identity. The artists created and shared artist statements about how their artwork addressed the inquiry question. So the art was a significant composition on its own, but then inspired writing in the informational and argument modes. Artwork in upper left explores how testing regimes "box" our identity. Artwork in upper right explores the archetypal energies that shape one's identity and uses a song lyric to express these energies. Artwork at right explores how popular cultural images of beauty affect our self-image.

CHAPTER 5

USING OUR LIVES TO SEE WHAT WE READ

Introductory Visualization Techniques

The CCSS bring into focus several understandings that have always been true, among them: literacy is essential to exercising one's full potential; everyone actually is held to the same standards out in the world; if we learn how to learn, then we can learn anything. It is now widely recognized that if a student struggles with reading (or writing or any other task), then it is our responsibility to help him or her. In this chapter, we will look at techniques that assist struggling readers to decode words and to "see" in order to comprehend what they read. Later in the chapter, I outline techniques that are helpful to readers of all abilities.

When my seventh graders arrived each day, I required them to show me the reading materials they had brought to class, give me a high five, and say "I am a reader!" or "I love reading!"

It was a fun ritual for most, but not for Marko. Each day he'd give me a high five and say something along the lines of "Reading is stupid!" or, on bad days, "Reading is for wusses!" Marko had one of the toughest shells I've ever had to crack. When I'd ask him to describe what he was seeing as he read, he couldn't do it. Working one-on-one with him, I discovered that he even had difficulty perceiving the actual words on the page. For example, when I asked him to tell me what he saw in a book about the Revolutionary War, he replied, "Just a bunch of black squiggles, like rabbit poop on the snow!"

We cannot read what we cannot see. This means students need to be able to perceive words and build visual meanings based on the ideas words and groups of words communicate and suggest to us.

It was then that I realized Marko was absolutely right in declaring that reading was stupid; for him, it was. To help Marko, I had to dig deep to help him "see" the actual words he was reading and then assist him in visualizing from these words. He didn't seem to have the vaguest notion of the end goal of reading—comprehending and making powerful meaning with text. I was badly out of my depth. I had to stretch my teaching repertoire, looking to both Marko and to various experts for ideas about how to help him. It was tough going, but in concert with some teachers who knew more than I did, Marko helped me to become a better teacher—one who could help him to become a better reader.

At the suggestion of our learning disabilities (LD) specialist, Judy Bovee, I asked our shop teacher to make a desktop sandbox in which both Marko and I could trace letters and words with our fingertips. I also brought in string that we used to create letters and words. These processes proved remarkably helpful in getting Marko to perceive unknown words and to be able to pronounce them, perhaps because they helped him to "see" the phonemes from which the words were made. But this was only the start. For the words to be meaningful, we now had to work on visualizing the meaning indicated by them. To this end, Marko and I sketched or acted out the meanings of words and phrases, created pictorial flash cards and grab bags, and engaged in many other visual activities.

Throughout our work together, I used the sociocultural scaffolding scheme of I DO/YOU WATCH, I DO/YOU HELP, YOU DO/I HELP, YOU DO/I WATCH. Because Marko was keen on car repair, we renamed the steps of this process as follows:

> Finding Our Bearings
>
> Getting Our Hands Dirty
>
> Making and Fixing It Together
>
> Doing It on My Own.

Marko had struggled for so long; I wanted to communicate that I would be with him every step of the way until he was ready to work on his own. For this reason, we focused on the "our" until he was ready for independence.

Marko was sometimes rambunctious and resistant, and our sessions often did not run smoothly. But after a semester of intense work, he was showing visible improvement as a reader. He certainly had a new understanding of what reading was and of himself as a reader, as evidenced by the fact that he often gave up lunch period for help with his reading. He also began to bring his reading materials to class, something he had resolutely refused to do earlier in the year. I realized that his resistance had been rooted in his feeling that he would never get the help he needed to become a reader. Once I convinced him that I would not give up on him, he began to show some enthusiasm for the project of learning to read. This was not a boy who resisted literacy. This was a boy who resisted failure and was angry about the lack of assistance available to him.

Letter From a Reader

I just read about writing in sand or with string and it brought back memories! I raised more than a few children of my own prior to teaching. Several of my children had motor skill and dyslexia challenges. Our OT, knowing I was working on my undergrad degree at the time, enlisted my help with a "play group" one son attended.

Addressing similar issues and gleaning the same results, I found using textured plexiglass worked well with my own kids (and since with the students I teach). The OT was pleased and sent me to have a set made. The plexiglass can be cut different sizes and shapes. The hardware store rounded the edges for me at no cost. Plexiglass comes in various textures. Words or images can be placed under the plexiglass and students can trace these with their fingers. A variety of materials may be used to trace on the plexiglass (naked fingers, pudding, some markers, powders, chalk...) as long as it can be cleaned off. You may have already come across this idea. However, I'm avoiding my homework and enjoying memories of some powerful teaching moments!

Thanks,

K.

Special Education, Head Swim Coach

In this chapter, I share some easy ways to get started with visualization strategies, whether you're teaching challenging students like Marko or proficient readers. I focus first on some of the word-level techniques that are effective for struggling readers, then proceed to techniques for helping students of all abilities to comprehend larger chunks of text.

Visualizing From Words: Suggested Activities

A basic ability for all readers, from elementary through high school, is the capacity to visualize the meanings of concepts or individual words. A scheme posed by the work of Fredericks (1986) and Barclay (1990) and based on the seminal work of Sadoski (1985) on visualization can help readers to achieve this. (A helpful summary of these schemes is provided in Gambrell & Koskinen, 2002.)

Anchor Standards
for Reading, 1, 4

Anchor Standards
for Language, 4–6

The seven-step sequence below is especially helpful to students at all ages and grade levels who, like Marko, may not yet be able to visually imagine at the word and local levels. For them, start with Step 1. For more accomplished readers, start later in the sequence, at their point of need.

Either in a whole-class setting or small groups, prompt students to:

Create mental images of observed concrete objects. Bring in interesting objects and have students handle, study, and carefully observe each object. Then have them close their eyes and imagine the most detailed version of the object that they can. Prompt them to describe the item to their classmates; other students can chime in with details they would add or change. Finally, have students open their eyes and compare their mental pictures and descriptions with the actual object they were attempting to imagine, noting how their vision and the object are similar and different. Emphasize that good readers use observed objects and visual experiences from their lives to form images as they read.

Create elaborate mental images of imagined concrete objects. Ask students to visualize an absent concrete object with which they have previous experience. Next, use guided imagery prompts to have them create ever more detailed visions of this object. For example, you could ask students to imagine a car, then provide additional specific details to get students to refine their visualization. You might prompt them to see a red sports car, or a red Corvette (just remember to choose something students are familiar with, if you want them to be specific), a shiny Corvette glistening with rain, a Corvette that is a convertible, with the top down, with white leather seats, and with its lights flashing. The point is to prompt students to move from imagining recently seen objects to visualizing objects by retrieving images from memory, and then refining and adapting these visions based on verbal cues. This prepares students to respond to cues in texts while reading and to continue to refine and build these images based on new and accumulating detail. This skill is an essential one that is gained by bringing visual experiences from one's life to the reading.

3 Envision familiar objects and settings from their own experience.
Next, prompt students to imagine familiar objects or scenes from home, such as the sugar jar in the kitchen, a clock, their bedroom, or a favorite place in their neighborhood. Invite them to sketch pictures and take them home to compare them to the actual objects or scenes, amending the drawings or adding details to them as they wish. You might also prompt students to use their perception of a bedroom or house and revise it to create a vision of a house or bedroom they have never seen, by using the kinds of prompts described in Step 2.

4 Add familiar actions and events, then relationships and settings.
Ask students to envision a familiar event or action, like a tea kettle whistling, or to run a brief video clip they have seen through their mind. Then ask them to build on an imagined object, such as the car described in Step 2, by visualizing it in a driveway on a sunny day, then pulling out of the driveway, squealing its wheels as it peels out, and stopping at a stop sign. Visualization skills are extended when students describe the relationship of the object to other objects or characters or put the object in motion or in a situation. The more sophisticated they become at envisioning, the more their visions will move and involve these kinds of relationships.

5 Picture characters, settings, details, and events while listening to a story read or told aloud. Read aloud imagery-intense narrative and expository texts about ideas that are familiar to students so that they will have images from their recent experiences to draw on as resources. Stop periodically to ask students to share their mental pictures; you might even ask them to identify what experiences they drew on to create their images. To extend this activity, have students work individually or in groups to create illustrations for each section of text.

6 Study text illustrations and use them to create internal images.
Discuss text illustrations of all kinds with students as you read with them. Discuss how illustrations work in various ways to give readers a sense of setting or context, characters, concepts, mood, interactions, relationships, actions, events, and trends. Explain that narratives ask us to visualize

a world and expository texts often ask us to create a mental model of a map, graph, or process. Think aloud about how you use such figures and illustrations to create your own mental pictures and models, and how you then use these mental representations to remember and think with. Prompt students to use text illustrations in the same ways. Explain that even when text illustrations are not available, their task as readers is to create the same kinds of visuals that would help them understand and manipulate textual ideas.

7 **Create mental pictures independently.** Prompt students to create mental pictures as they read on their own. (If students cannot do this, work with them using the prior activities in this seven-step sequence.) I've found it effective to invite students to create journal entries or drawings that respond to prompts I provide at strategic points in a text.

Remember that you might choose to start at different points of this sequence with different students, depending on what they already do as readers. More engaged readers might only need Step 7, but readers who struggle will benefit from the whole sequence. Once a student "gets it," move on to challenge him or her in another way by using ideas from a subsequent step.

Especially for Struggling Readers

Nanci Bell (1991) provides a particularly effective scheme to assist struggling readers, one that is consistent with the seven-step sequence above. She argues that an essential part of reading is the ability to create a "Gestalt," or a visual sense of a whole scene, idea, or plot progression. Her findings are in line with my own classroom data (Wilhelm, 1995, 1997/2008): Highly engaged, successful readers see details, ideas, and scenes and are able to blend these together into an organic and dynamic whole. This synthesizing process has many benefits for the reader. Bell cites Long, Winograd, and Bridge (1989):

> Imagery may be involved in the reading process in a number of ways. First, imagery may increase the capacity of working memory during reading by assimilating details and propositions into chunks which are carried along during reading. Second, imagery seems to be involved in making comparisons or analogies—that is, in matching schematic and textual information. Third, imagery seems to function as an organizational tool for coding and storing meaning from the reading. (Bell, 1991, pg. 250)

In Bell's scheme, students are helped to visualize the meaning represented by written words. They are assisted, one on one, in moving from "word imaging" to "single sentence imaging" to "sentence by sentence imaging" with oral and then written language. Eventually, students are assisted in handling multiple-sentence imaging, whole-paragraph imaging, and paragraph-by-paragraph imaging. A unique part of Bell's program is the use of "structure word" prompts. As a resource for creating rich visions, readers use cards with prompts, like *what*, *where*, and *when*, as well as more specific words, like *size*, *shape*, and *movement*, and synesthetic elements, like mood. Students refer to the cards while visualizing to help them refine their visualization.

Bell's research involved intense treatment: four hours of daily work with students for a total of nearly 48 hours. She established that this intense work resulted in statistically significant increases in comprehension for readers from elementary school to retirement age. Her book *Visualizing and Verbalizing* (1991) is highly recommended by my colleagues in special education who have used her technique to great effect.

Activities for Word-Level Visualization

Students who have great difficulty perceiving individual words and stitching them together to comprehend a text's meaning benefit from individual and small-group work with the activities listed below. Notice that these activities are ways of localizing and intensifying the work described in Step 1 of the seven-step sequence I described earlier.

Writing in Sand or With String

Have students trace words in a small sandbox or give them string, clay, and pipe cleaners and have them form words with these materials. These two techniques were remarkably successful with Marko. Judy Bovee, the learning specialist who recommended them to me, felt that Marko was so profoundly LD that he needed a visual and kinesthetic experience of words before he would remember and recognize them. Young children are often given these tactile experiences; teachers of older struggling readers aren't as likely to know about these techniques.

Consider This

Rudolf Arnheim, a pioneer of visual psychology, asserts that behind every word is some kind of image. The history of written language began with pictographs that drew on this direct relationship. In English we use the "phonetic rebus" principle, which allows us to use symbols for their phonetic value. But students can still use the intimate connection between words and images to help them comprehend and create meaning with words.

Drawing Word Representations

When students have difficulty imagining a particular noun or verb, it is often helpful to ask them to visualize a noun or verb that is familiar to them. You can then ask them specific questions about attributes, such as color, size, context, motion, effect, or emotion, until you can draw the specific picture they are envisioning. Build on this by giving students the information they need to visualize the meaning of an unfamiliar word until they can make a drawing that captures the central meaning of that word.

Picture Flash Cards

Ask students to write a word on one side of an index card. On the other side, have them draw a picture or use a clip art image that in some way captures the word's meaning. Ask students to explain how their image connects to the word's meaning. To extend the activity, have students include a written definition, a synonym, or an antonym of the word.

A picture flash card of the term *nebula*.

Information Gap Activity

In this activity, one student knows something that his or her classmates do not, and this student is asked to convey what he or she knows to others. I learned of this concept from Karl Androes of Chicago's Reading in Motion, who came across it in *Games for Language Learning* by Andrew Wright, David Bettridge, and Michael Buckby. It's a great way to add suspense to language lessons. For example, in Karl's dance-based work with younger students on phonemic awareness and the alphabetic principle, the teacher whispers a word or nonsense word into the ear of a student (or to a small group) who is designated as the performer. The performer's task is to figure out what letters represent the spoken sounds of that word and how to make those letter shapes with his body in order to spell the word correctly. The performer then performs the word for the rest of the class, who must guess the word the performer is spelling. Students love trying to be the first to guess the word. This activity can also be used to portray concepts, ideas, and scenes through illustrating the meaning or aspects of the term.

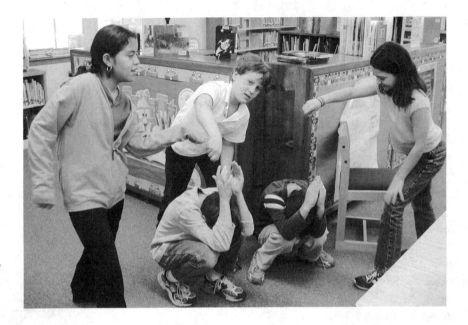

Vocabulary tableau: Students perform the meaning of the word oppression.

Vocabulary Tableaux

Jamie Heans, formerly a teacher in Brewer, Maine (at the professional development network site where I worked for several years), uses this and the following two techniques to teach new vocabulary. Tableau is the French word for "visual presentation," so a "vocabulary tableau" is a visual presentation of a relevant vocabulary word. A vocabulary tableau might be a mural, a chalk drawing on the board, or a pose or dance. Students might be asked to create a simple statue or a statue with a commentary or epitaph to illustrate a word. Or they might create a moving statue, photograph, or short video clip (which is particularly useful in describing an action or process). Jamie often assigns student groups to "perform" different vocabulary terms. For example, for a unit on survival, students might perform the meaning of the term *symbiosis* by showing a group working together, or perform the word *niche* by having one student occupy a space no one else enters as they go about their business around the first student (see Wilhelm, 2002, 2007).

Vocabulary PowerPoint

Jamie sometimes asks his students to create quick PowerPoint slides of vocabulary words, having them illustrate word meanings through clip art, photographs found in magazines or taken with a digital camera, embedded video (found or created), animation, and music. PowerPoint and its equivalents (like Apple's Keynote) are very simple forms of presentation software that many kids already know how to use or can learn within a class period. I have watched Jamie's students create vocabulary and terminology slides in less than ten minutes. A slide show of the whole class's efforts can be created and shared within a 40-minute period and made available as an electronic reference or glossary throughout a unit.

Video Clips for Summarizing

Students often have difficulty grasping the basic facts of a story or text and then putting these into the right sequence or another kind of meaningful pattern. To help your students build this vital skill, have them create short videos of the major scenes or ideas of a text in a meaningful sequence. Encourage them to make their video summaries as brief as possible—this activity is meant to be quick, easy, and somewhat spontaneous. This is tableaux vivant, a technique I describe in the drama/action strategies book in this series.

Video Clips for Exploring Literary Devices

Assign small student groups a literary device and a scene from a book the class is reading. Each group's task is to create a video that defines the device, then display the technique in action in a scene they have read. Videos conclude with a commentary on how the device helps to create meaning. For example, I recently watched a group of Jamie's students make a video defining the term *soliloquy* during a single class period. They did so with great humor, first querying two students about the meaning of the term. One said, "Uhhh… I really have absolutely no idea." The next student fabricated a definition, claiming that a soliloquy was a rare African silkworm. Then the group inserted a clip that reads "Actually… " and offered the correct definition. They then performed a scene with a person speaking thoughts aloud as if no one else could hear, and explained that a soliloquy helps readers to understand a scene in a play by allowing them to read or hear the character's thoughts. When the class had finished the book they were working on, they compiled their work into a video glossary of literary terms that included how the terms were put to use by the author. This is one of my favorite visualization activities, because kids are so highly engaged by it and often create hilarious or poignant movies. And because the videos are shown to the rest of the class as soon as they are made, they enhance the discussion of the text and boost every reader's understanding.

> **Michael Smith's Rules for Drama Work**
> - Short
> - Scriptless
> - Spontaneous
> - Not Seldom!

Games

Games like Pictionary™ or Cranium™, which require students to draw ideas, vocabulary, or concepts, are both fun and excellent at stimulating visualization. I have such games in my room and often play one with students during lunch or encourage them to do so during study hall, if they have no homework.

Techniques for Visualizing Across Texts

Of course, being able to comprehend and visualize word meanings and central concepts is essential to reading. As necessary as this skill is, by itself it is not sufficient for achieving an expert level of reading. Students must learn to coherently envision chunks of text as organic meanings.

In addition to using many of the ideas cited above, I also took care to do a lot of reading to and for Marko, then with him, before I asked him to read on his own. I usually read a text to him and then used the activities above to do "word work" with a few words from the reading. This helped him to remember that the skills we were learning were not decontextualized but should be put to use in real reading situations to make meaning, and that the ultimate end of our project was for him to be able to read on his own.

While I was working with Marko, who was a big sports fan, I brought in the newspaper every day and we read the sports page together. This had a huge unintended benefit. As we often read about sporting events that Marko had attended or games he had watched on TV, he was assisted in visualizing the scenes and events described in the stories: He could use his memory of actually seeing the events instead of having to imagine them from scratch. Also, instead of feeling that Marko's attendance at sports events and his television viewing were taking away from his study time, I was able to use it as a resource to help him improve as a reader. I also taught Marko how to search the Internet, and we bookmarked several Milwaukee Brewers, Green Bay Packers, and Wisconsin Badgers websites on which we could monitor stories about his favorite teams.

These activities gave me a sense of déjà vu. I was helped through some reading difficulties myself in second grade by one of the greatest teachers I have ever known. His name was Orlando Schultz, and he claimed that he "could teach anybody to read through one interest." Orlando often taught kids to read with the newspaper by having them follow stories or issues that were of passionate interest to them. And this is what I found myself doing with Marko: teaching him a foundational set of strategies in reading by using the sports he was so interested in.

With Marko, as I would with other struggling readers, I moved from read-alouds and guided imagery with texts we read and reread together (shown to have significant benefits at all grade levels and with all abilities of students; see Sulzby, 1985) to providing visual prompts with reading we did together or that he did on his own. This allowed him to practice becoming adept at using imagery in independent reading situations.

Pushing Beyond Prompts

Various studies have demonstrated that simply suggesting to students that they attempt to form visual images as they read improves engagement, comprehension, and comprehension monitoring. It seems that most younger readers do not spontaneously employ imagery as a reading strategy, and yet many have the capacity to do so when prompted (Gambrell and Koskinen, 2002). However, my own studies (Wilhelm 1995; 1997/2208) and those of others, have found that many struggling readers do not employ imagery and do not know how to do so. Simply prompting them will not suffice. These readers need scaffolded assistance with visualization strategies. Even more accomplished readers can improve their visualization skills through scaffolded help, which deepens their engagement, comprehension, and ability to learn and use ideas.

It is therefore important to explicitly identify the use of visual strategies to create mental imagery as an essential part of reading. It helps readers to experience stories and other textual information and think about the content of the text.

Consider This

While it sounds a bit like a template for a blues song, this mnemonic is a way to think about how to gradually release responsibility for using a new strategy to students.

Aloud: Use and model the technique for students. Do it by reading aloud and making the technique visible.

Along: Then do it along with students.

Alone: When they are ready, ask them to do it alone, but be ready to help.

As you read aloud, identify the cues you use to create a "story world."

Read-Alouds and Think-Alouds to Model Imagery (I Do/You Watch)

Reading aloud to students is a great way to help them build their image-making abilities. As you read aloud, be sure you also think aloud to model how you create images as you read. Use texts that are rich in images, and then demonstrate several times how you create images. Below is an example of how I think aloud during a read-aloud. I often teach a unit on civil rights around the question "What are civil rights, and how can we protect them?" One of my favorite texts to use in this unit is *Leon's Story* (1997) by Leon Walter Tillage (who just happened to be the janitor at the school where my wife first taught!). It's a fabulous story and has beautiful collage art by Susan Roth. Her images symbolize the meaning of Leon's various experiences. This kind of thematic visualization is very helpful to students wrestling with the deep implications of Leon's story. It gives me an opportunity to think aloud about the illustrations and their relationship to the story's meaning, and it gives my students a model of how to use visuals to reinforce thematic implications. This is how I start:

Okay, is everybody on page 5 of *Leon's Story*? I look at this collage and I think, it's just row after row of corn. Wow, that must be a lot of work to farm. There's just corn everywhere. It makes me think that maybe Leon's life as a sharecropper was just working in the fields with no time for anything else. In fact, the corn looks like prison bars.

All right, on page 7, let's read together: "We lived on a farm owned by Mr. Johnson. He had lots of acres and grew lots of different crops—corn, tobacco, cotton, alfalfa, wheat, and sometimes sugarcane. It was mostly cotton and tobacco, though, because in those days those were the number one crops."

In my mind, I see this big farmhouse where Mr. Johnson lives. I see it as well kept and painted white with black shutters and a big front porch with a swing. I imagine this because Leon says Mr. Johnson owned the farm, and, because I grew up on a farm, I can use the farmhouses I know to imagine what Mr. Johnson's might look like. In my mind, surrounding the house are fields as far as you can see, full of corn with tassels, big-leafed tobacco plants, and cotton with the cotton balls at the end of branches. I can see all this because these are the crops Leon mentions, because I know what cornfields look like, and because I was once in the south and saw cotton and tobacco farms. I know tobacco looks like this (I draw a picture) and cotton plants look like this (I draw a picture). If I hadn't seen the plants before, I would try to imagine what they might look like or would Google an image.

I also see the decrepit house Leon says they live in: no paint, grey, sagging roof and porch. I see an aerial view of the farm and how these shacks are spread around at the edge of

continued next page

Leon's Story

LEON WALTER TILLAGE
Collage art by Susan L. Roth

Sharecropping

We lived on a farm owned by Mr. Johnson. He had lots of acres and grew lots of different crops—corn, tobacco, cotton, alfalfa, wheat, and sometimes sugarcane. It was mostly cotton and tobacco, though, because in those days those were the number one crops.

My father was a sharecropper, which means he had to share half of everything he had with Mr. Johnson. So, let's say Mr. Johnson gave my father ten acres of tobacco, ten

7

Build a collection of books that have powerful visuals.

continued from previous page

Mr. Johnson's fields. I think I get the images of the shacks from WPA photographs I have seen. I often use photos or movies I know to help me see what I am reading. And if I don't remember any images, I might try to find some photos on the Internet. (With my digital projector, I show them some photos from the WPA and Smithsonian collections.) You can do a quick Google search and get help visualizing scenes you might not know much about. (I draw a quick sketch of Mr. Johnson's big house, surrounded by crops and, at the edges, little shacks for the sharecroppers.)

Okay, let's continue reading: "My father was a sharecropper, which means he had to share half of everything with Mr. Johnson. So let's say Mr. Johnson gave my father ten acres of corn—whatever—to work. Then, at the end of the year, when it came time to sell the crops and settle up, Mr. Johnson would get five acres of each crop and my father would get the other five."

You know, now I am thinking of the collage that started this chapter and how much corn there was. I'm thinking about how much work it must have taken to plant, and to harvest, and then to cut down the stalks and clear the fields. And I take half of the harvest away—but none of the work. I see a bar graph in my mind. One bar is the amount of corn ten acres would produce. Below it is another bar that is half as long, which is the corn Leon and his father would get. (I draw my graph on the board, labeling each line.) This is called making a mental model of the meaning of what you are reading. Okay, back to Leon:

"Maybe it sounds good, but the problem was my father had to pay Mr. Johnson for supplies and such, and he purchased the food we'd needed to live on for the past year on credit from the corner store. So out of our half he needed to pay off those debts. . . . At the end of the year, we'd settle our debts. Then Mr. Johnson would say to my father, 'Well, Ivory, you almost got out of debt that time. I think next year you'll make it.'"

In my mind, I see Leon's father giving Mr. Johnson half the corn, then the other half of the corn to pay off his debts, and then Mr. Johnson telling him he is still in debt. I change the graph in my mind so that there is no bar for the corn that Leon and his father would get, and a long bar representing all of the corn going to Mr. Johnson. (I change my graph on the board.) And I see how Leon and his father have done all the work and gotten none of the corn. All they have earned is enough food to survive, and they are still indebted to Mr. Johnson, so they have to keep working for him next year. In my mind, the scene with Mr. Johnson and Leon and his father takes on a red tint because I am sure Leon and his father are being cheated and I am angry about that. Okay, we're going to continue reading, but now I want you to visualize in your mind what *you* see. I'd like you to be able to tell a partner what words from the text help you to see what Leon describes, and what experiences from your life help you to see it. If you can't see it, think of where you could find some pictures or have some experiences that would help you to see it.

As you read and think aloud, identify the cues that you use to begin creating a "story world" (for a narrative) or a "mental model" of the information, concepts, or processes (for both narrative and informational text). You might even choose to draw quick sketches of your story world or mental model and share them with students. Be sure to identify the cues that prompted you and the life experiences you used to build the images the way you did. If I can, I provide students with a short excerpt of the text that I will think aloud with and have them circle or underline the visual cues I use to make my mental images. Later on in the process, I ask students to circle their own clues, first with my help, then on their own.

As you do this kind of thinking aloud and visual prompting, you might focus on particular techniques the author uses, conventions of particular kinds of texts (such as classification, argument, and expository writings), or conventions that run across texts (such as symbolism, irony, and unreliable narrators). In my classroom, I use lots of expository texts for read-alouds and think-alouds—including primary source materials, nonfiction, and historical texts—because these can be challenging for young readers who are used to reading fictional narrative. For example, I might read aloud from great children's or young adult books like *Dolphin Man* (Pringle, 2003) to show how gripping quotes are used to put readers in the midst of the action. *Phineas Gage* (Fleischman, 2002) starts with a description of Phineas using the tamping iron that explodes through his brain but does not kill him or destroy his intellectual functions. The author prompts readers to visualize and live through the incredible scene that was the beginning of modern brain science. Jim Murphy's *Across America on an Emigrant Train* (1993) uses a real diary entry to open each chapter, establishing the historical situation and personal context. When I highlight the features of such texts—including their use of quotation, historical anecdote, and primary source materials—I help students to see how authors use particular techniques to help their audience see and experience what they are reading. In turn, students learn how to craft their own writing to shape the experience of an audience.

Read-Alouds and Guided Imagery (I Do/You Help)

The next step to induce students to create images is to prompt them as they listen to you read either stories or informational text. Instead of creating or describing the images yourself, cite the prompts you have noticed and ask students to create and describe their visualizations to the class, small groups, or partners. Provide assistance as needed by asking for justifications based on text cues or by correcting misconceptions, if students bring inconsistent images to bear. Have students compare and contrast the images they have created, and compare the textual cues and life experiences they used to create such images.

It is important when using guided imagery and think-alouds to identify the visual and descriptive cues you use to see what you read. These stimulate image-making, helping students to notice and use these cues on their own.

The research makes it clear both that imagery is an essential part of the expert reader's repertoire and that many students need very explicit and active teacher support to internalize this strategy for themselves. Repeated practice and prompting will help students to develop the skill of creating images based on text cues, and will help them to do this habitually. It is important for us as teachers to stress that valid images depend both on the reader's experience and on textual cues, and that the actual image depends on the active engagement of the reader.

Simple Prompting (You Do/I Help)

Eventually, you can read aloud, or have students read aloud to each other, and simply prompt them to circle visual cues and make pictures in their heads about story events or ideas. With some readers, simple prompting will suffice to help them visualize. Using the techniques described in this chapter will help even struggling readers eventually progress to the point where you can simply prompt them, then intervene as necessary. As always, teaching interventions should be used only if and when needed by particular students or groups of students. Often, a technique will be helpful to everyone in a class. Sometimes, the level of support or way the technique is used will vary between classroom groups. At other times, perhaps only a few students will require the

Basic Ways to Conduct Think-Alouds

- Teacher does think-aloud; students listen. Teacher identifies particular cues and strategies to use in response to these cues. (Sets of cues can be identified that are related to any purpose or convention, including those cited in the CCSS).

- Teacher does think-aloud; students help out.

- Students do think-alouds as large group; teacher and other students monitor and help.

- Students do think-alouds as small group; teacher and other students monitor and help.

- Individual student does think-aloud in forum; other students help.

- Students do think-aloud individually; compare with others.

For more on using the think-aloud strategy, see *Improving Comprehension With Think-Aloud Strategies* (Wilhelm, 2012).

intervention. It all depends on your students' zones of proximal development. Luckily, all the techniques offered here are flexible and can be pitched to readers at almost any level of expertise. Below are prompts to share with your students.

Some General Visualization Prompts

- As you read, make pictures in your mind to help you understand and remember.

- Try to build images of people, places, interactions, events, processes, and ideas as you read.

- Use memories and objects from your life experience to "see" what you are reading.

- Make a movie in your mind as you read.

- Try to recall the major scene, main idea, important process, and so on, from your reading by using an image or moving images.

- Use visuals to place-hold major ideas and their sequence.

- Explain how and why visions or pictures develop and change with the introduction of new information.

Some Prompts for Seeing the "Story World"

- What impressions are forming in your mind of the people and settings?

- Where does the story take place? What is it like there? What kinds of buildings, trees, and so on, do you see?

- Does it matter where the story takes place? Could it take place elsewhere or anywhere? Does it matter when the story happens? Is the historical situation important or could the events happen at any time in any place?

- Does it matter from what perspective you see the story? How would the story and what you see as the reader be different if it were told from another viewpoint?

- How do you respond to the setting as you read? How does it make you feel? How does it compare to what you know?

- If you were going to take a picture or make a movie of a particular scene, where in our community would you stage it? What props would you include? What sort of music would you be playing?

Anchor Standards
for Reading, 1–6

Anchor Standard
for Writing, 4

- What do the characters look like? How are they dressed or groomed? How do they walk, stand, gesture, interact, or display emotions? What classmates or famous actors would you cast for each part and why?

- Where are the characters in relationship to each other? To the setting? To objects in the setting? (This gives you the chance to use maps and tableaux.)

- What helps you to see pictures of characters, scenes, events, and ideas? How and when does the clarity of your vision change? From what perspective or position are you seeing the story?

- What kinds of details help you to envision the story? How are these connected to your life or reading experiences?

- What other ways do you see or sense the story world?

- If you were to create a symbol or object to represent the mood of this scene, what would it be? How would you create a symbol of the deep meaning or theme of the scene? How would you symbolize a message about human behavior that we could use in our lives?

Visual Think-Alouds

A favorite technique of mine is to have students sketch anything they see, think, or feel as they go through a think-aloud of a text (Wilhelm, 2001/2012). I often type an excerpt of text on the left-hand side of a sheet of paper and have students draw their responses on the right side, next to the textual cues that stimulated these responses. At other times I provide students with sheets of paper and ask them to sketch their

Denali creates a visual think-aloud to explore her response to a book.

visualizations at particular points in the story. I sometimes have them do a back-to-back description: I ask them to identify the visual cues and structure-words that helped them to visualize the particular image or scene they sketched. They then list these cues on the back of their pictures so the relationship between verbal stimuli and visual response can be seen. In other words, students see how the cues, their experiences, and their resulting visual representations are all connected.

I left New York in May. I had a penknife, a ball of cord, an ax, and $40, which I had saved from selling magazine subscriptions. I also had some flint and steel which I had bought at a Chinese store in the city. The man in the store had showed me how to use it. He had also given me a little purse to put it in and some tinder to catch the sparks. He had told me that if I ran out of tinder, I should burn cloth, and use the charred ashes.

I thanked him and said, "This is the kind of thing that I am not going to forget."

On the train north to the Catskills I unwrapped my flint and steel and practiced hitting them together to make sparks. On the wrapping paper I made these notes.

"A hard brisk strike is best. Remember to hold the steel in the left hand and the flint in the right, and hit the steel with the flint.

"The trouble is the sparks go every which way."

And that *was* the trouble. I did not get a fire going that night, and as I mentioned, this was a scary experience.

A visual think-aloud for *My Side of the Mountain* by Jean Craighead George.

Embracing "Alternative" Texts and Literacies

In the review of studies *Achieving Literacy* (Meek et al., 1983), Margaret Meek describes how she assisted illiterate seventh graders in becoming engaged readers through the intense one-on-one reading of picture books. Many of my own most reluctant readers can remember neither having picture books read to them nor reading such books. Such texts, of course, directly connect text to images, communicate the idea that reading is a visual experience, and improve facility at creating such images in one's mind. I encourage you to embrace many forms of texts that combine words and pictures and graphics, including graphic novels, magazines, journals, websites, multimedia texts, age-appropriate comic books, sophisticated textbooks, and so on.

Picture Books

I often start a unit by reading picture books, even with my middle and high school students. This provides everyone with a successful reading experience, puts them all in the game, and provides a basic shared background experience. During a recent unit on the

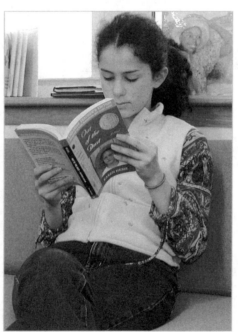

A student reads *Out of the Dust* by Karen Hesse.

Great Depression, my middle schoolers read illustrated books, such as Jerry Stanley's magnificent *Children of the Dust Bowl* and Ann Turner's *Dust for Dinner*. Some students, for whom this reading was appropriately challenging, continued to read these sophisticated kinds of picture books and searched the Internet to find information and images (see, for example, www.scs.state. mi.us/history/ museum/ kidstuff/depression/ costlist.html) to create original picture books that could become classroom resources. Other students went on to read Karen Hesse's *Out of the Dust*, Richard Peck's *A Year Down Yonder*, Christopher Paul Curtis's *Bud, Not Buddy*, or David Booth's *The Dust Bowl*. Everyone was reading a text that was appropriately challenging, and everyone could participate fully and equally in the classroom project of studying the Depression and answering our inquiry questions about people's experiences of that time. It all began by reading picture books.

Graphic novels

There are also many wonderful graphic novels or manga that are worthy of study in their own right, or that can also be used as the initial text in a sequence of readings throughout an inquiry. I have had great luck introducing Holocaust units with the now classic Maus books: *Maus I* and *Maus II* by Art Spiegelman. I have also used *Persepolis* by Marjane Satrapi in inquiry units about questions around culture: "How does culture shape identity?" and civil rights: "What protects and promotes civil rights?" and others, as well as *American Born Chinese* by Gene Luen Yang for various identity units: "How does culture shape identity?" and "What makes me me?" There are many great graphic novels and works of manga.

Overlay Maps

During a unit I helped to plan with teachers at the Chicago Teachers Center, Chicago students read Jim Murphy's books *The Blizzard* (a fascinating story of a debilitating blizzard in New York City that led to the establishment of the National Weather Bureau) and *The Great Fire* (see also www.chicagohs.org/fire) as an introduction to how accounts of disasters can vary. Students created an overlay map: a map of Chicago at the time of the fire

Resources

Following are some powerful books that make use of visuals:

Avi's futuristic myth *City of Light; City of Dark*.

Robert Burleigh's *Into the Air* about the Wright Brothers' first flight.

Steven Kellogg's folklore comic book *Mike Fink*.

Mordicai Gerstein's *What Charlie Heard* explores visual connections to Charles Ives' music.

Jan Greenberg's *Action Jackson* about the artist Jackson Pollock explores how people see.

James Rumford's stunning book *Traveling Man*, about a 14th-century Muslim pilgrim who walked 70,000 miles, uses illuminated Arabic verses from the Koran— useful for units on culture, the hero quest, or the human journey.

Lists such as the Orbis Pictus Awards for children's literature and your library media specialist are great resources for finding such books.

overlaying a current map of Chicago. They colored in places that burned as they read the story, adding notes or pictures about important places, people, and events as they read about them.

Watching Video Excerpts

In a listserv discussion, the noted researcher Judith Langer asserted that using videos could assist students in developing what she calls "envisionment-building stances." She explained that some students are so distant from the language, social situation, settings, or other aspects of a written text that they will have great difficulty "stepping into an envisionment"—a prerequisite for all further engagement and reflection on the text. Scaffolding can be provided by using a video to create some visual images, as sense of setting, time period, character, plot, or language, that will help students envision the text. Even short clips may be enough to help students envision the written text.

Lunch Club Videos: Reading Captions

For a couple of years, I invited a group of students who struggled with reading to a lunch club. We munched our sandwiches in my room while we watched videos. We'd watch one of their choice, then one of mine (which would be associated with a unit we were pursuing or a book we were reading). The catch was that there was no sound; students had to read the captions at the bottom of the screen. I found this to be a highly engaging way to get them to read text in a manner that was supported by visual images.

What's at Stake?

Anchor Standard for Reading, 7

Anchor Standard for Writing, 8

The research on boys and literacy that I conducted with my colleague Michael Smith (Smith & Wilhelm, 2002, 2006) has convinced me that we need to use a wide variety of visual and nonvisual popular-culture texts in the classroom—because these "texts" are worthy of study and critique in themselves—and also serve as a bridge to more traditional forms of text, and help expand our notions of literacy and text. We found that boys rejected the "schoolishness" of school reading, which they saw as totally divorced from the literacy and concerns that they practiced in their own lives. Bringing in popular-culture texts communicated that the class project would both value and include their literacies and allow them to use these literacies as a resource and bridge to developing more academic literacies. The boys can therefore see a way to bring preexisting interests and competence to school literacies that typically cause them difficulty. Such a project also helps us to expand our notion of what counts as a text. The boys were cynical about school because schools place a high—and nearly exclusive value—on long texts such as textbooks, novels, and plays when these were unlike the texts they used in their lives, which were increasingly short, electronic, and multimedia. Finally, given the challenges of navigating various literacies in everyday life, the literacies in academic and disciplinary work, as well as those offered by the Common Core, we need to use all resources and tools at our disposal to help our students to meet them.

Expanding our notions of text and literacy, and then using these wider views to help students gain new literacies can be powerful, particularly for our most disenfranchised students.

FROM THE KNOWN TO THE NEW

Building Background Before and During Reading

Americans of my generation, we often ask one another where they were when they heard that John F. Kennedy had been assassinated. I remember sitting on my mother's lap in front of our small black and white television, and I remember her body heaving as she sobbed. Today, we might ask students where they were on 9/11. Yet when the Seal 6 team recently succeeded in their mission to find and capture Osama bin Laden, that evil architect of 9/11, most of the ninth graders I was working with professed to have no actual memory of that day. None remembered the Taliban's takeover in Afghanistan, or the Christmas Island refugees that were part of the run-up to 9/11. This brought back vivid memories of an afternoon in 1987 when I was teaching Tom Wolfe's *The Right Stuff* to my ninth grade

English class. One boy asked me what the term "Watergate" referred to. I shunted the question to the rest of the class. No one responded. "Come on, people!" I cried. "Nineteen-seventy-two! Richard Nixon's resignation, the erased tapes, the Watergate Hotel! Come on! Let's open those memory banks!" Jamie Delikowski raised his hand and said, "Mr. Wilhelm, none of us were born in 1972, so we can't remember any of that." I was stunned, but a quick mathematical calculation showed me that Jamie was right.

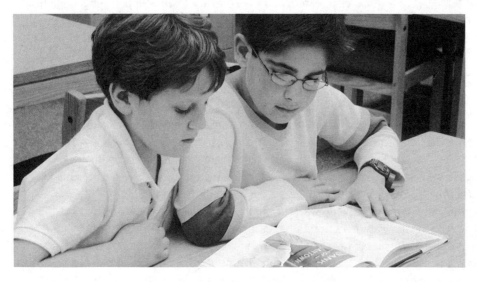

Readers are engaged by topics and settings that are familiar.

I've experienced many moments like this, when my students shocked me with what they didn't yet know, as well as many when they amazed me with what they did know. These experiences have taught me the importance of activating and teasing out what students know and don't know before starting a unit. Otherwise, time gets wasted and students get frustrated. But it wasn't until Michael Smith and I embarked on our literacy research (Smith & Wilhelm, 2002, 2006) that the vital role of accessing and building knowledge prior to reading really sunk in.

Examining boys' reading habits taught us just how powerful the familiar is to engagement and comprehension. For example, the boys from Maine we studied enjoyed or gravitated toward books about Maine or the Maritime provinces. *Lost on a Mountain in Maine* (Fendler, 1978) was a favorite book of many students, who talked about having seen or climbed Mount Katahdin, which helped them connect to and enjoy the book. *The Perfect Storm* (Junger, 1999) and *The Hungry Ocean* (Greenlaw, 2000) were free-reading choices of many of these boys due to their familiarity with settings on or off the coast of Maine. They enjoyed reading the poems of Maine poet Paul Corrigan from *At the Grave of the Unknown Riverdriver* (1984) because they recognized the places and the activities he described.

The Assessment Bonus

The techniques introduced in this chapter can serve as pre-assessments to help you plan instruction. They reveal what students know and need to know, so you can teach more effectively.

These boys were passionate about the issue of overfishing lobster, a huge debate in that part of the state. They eagerly read *Cod* (Kurlansky, 2003), *The Lobster Chronicles* (Greenlaw, 2002), and many other difficult texts related to this issue. Other boys in the study, whether living in rural, suburban, or urban areas, responded strongly to the familiar, too.

Michael Smith and I were struck by how important geographical locations were to the boys' engagement with reading. To be sure, this finding isn't earthshaking—it's supported by the last 30-plus years of research in cognition—but it resonated with us. The boys we studied embraced books whose terrain was as familiar as the floorboards of their houses or the lobster boats bobbing in the harbor. Put more pedagogically, these books allowed the boys to bring to the text all the details that "connect the dots" and make the text meaningful. They could read with ease, confidence, and enjoyment.

In other words, it wasn't just the topics that were compelling; these books were smooth, satisfying rides. They made the boys feel competent as readers because they didn't have to struggle to comprehend them.

We wondered what to do with this finding. How do we as teachers harness the power of the familiar, of a priori interests and knowledge, in order to stretch students, to get them to embrace new challenges and master new concepts and strategies as readers and thinkers? That's what this chapter explores. In it, I share with you "frontloading" techniques that use visuals to build new images and schema before reading, so that children never come to a text cold. Instead, they'll arrive with a sense of being on familiar terrain, with the resources they need to be successful.

The Benefits of Frontloading: Preparing Students for Success

In terms of the scaffolding metaphor, frontloading activates and makes visible the foundation of prior experience. New meanings are built on this foundation, and all future learning of more complex versions of the concept depend upon first creating that firm foundation. Frontloading techniques accomplish the following:

- Connect to prior interests and stir children's curiosity about a text.

- Trigger the appropriate background knowledge that students already possess.

- Build on and "load up" students' minds with the knowledge they need to comprehend the text.

- Provide a scaffold and template that organizes the experience and learning that accrues through reading, allowing it to be added to prior knowledge and existing schema.

Frontloading occurs at the beginning of a unit or reading but is referred to continually throughout a reading until individual students have mastered the independent use of the knowledge. Without frontloading, students' comprehension never engages and can often collapse. For example, on one memorable occasion, I was co-teaching a science unit on enzymes. The lead teacher began the unit by having students read the chapter in the textbook. She then gave a quiz on the chapter that nearly everyone in the class failed.

"What went wrong?" she asked me.

"Well," I began, "they don't know anything about enzymes."

"That's why I assigned them to read the chapter!" she protested. "To introduce them to the basic ideas!"

"But they can't read the text purposefully or comprehend it if they don't know something about enzymes first, or why they should want to know it!"

"Well, how do you ever get started, then?" she asked me.

"We have to give them concrete experiences with enzymes—do experiments, show a video, talk about enzymes and enzymatic reactions in the home..."

After engaging them in these hands-on experiences, our students' interest was much higher and comprehension significantly improved. In fact, the students were able to compose maps and flow charts describing how enzymes work that showed deep understanding.

When I work with teachers, I want them to absolutely remember a few key things, no matter what. One of them is this: The most important time to teach anything—but particularly reading—is before kids start to learn something new or to read a text that presents them with a new challenge.

Transactional theories of reading, schema theory, and three decades of cognitive research explain why this is true: The reader must bring meaning and strategies to bear on a text in order to be able to comprehend it.

Trina whispers to Josh the meaning of a good relationship after posting her ideas. Frontloading techniques such as this serve as a gateway to understanding new concepts and strategies. These students were about to launch into a unit on the topic of good relationships.

Getting Started: Frontloading Activities

All the frontloading activities presented below are consistent with the Vygotskian injunction that learning must proceed from the known to the new and from the concrete to the abstract. The first is an activity that underlies all of the others and perhaps lives up to the spirit Vygotsky and Dewey best of all: providing students with firsthand experiences.

Firsthand Experiences

Research in emergent literacy shows that the most powerful thing we can do to support children in becoming readers is to provide them with a wide variety of life experiences. These life experiences create interests and background knowledge (schema) that empower readers. Introductory field trips, classroom demonstrations, visual aids, drama work, simulations, flow charts, maps, video viewing, and many other experiences are therefore excellent frontloading activities. They provide and build background knowledge students need in order to read particular texts or to pursue thematic inquiries.

When I taught in Baltimore, my school began the year with class field trips to build up instructional support for future learning. Each year, I led a group of tenth graders on a bike trip through Civil War sites that took us backwards from the Confederacy's high point to the beginning of the war. We watched the movie *Gettysburg* before we departed. We then followed the route of J. E. B. Stuart's cavalry through Maryland to Gettysburg. Once there, we surveyed the battlefield as if we were Meade's first scouts. We attempted to find strategic advantage. We camped behind the Confederate lines and discussed what our own strategy would have been. The next day, we took a tour of the battlefield, biked the battle lines of each of the battle's three days, and ultimately ran the downhill bayonet charge of the 20th Maine regiment on Little Round Top and walked the route of Pickett's charge. We then biked down to the Antietam battlefield and to the site in Harper's Ferry where Colonel Robert E. Lee captured John Brown. We moved on from there to Manasses (or Bull Run, if you are a Southerner), site of the first significant battle of the war.

Upon our return we engaged in a study of politics, power, and history through the American Civil War. We asked: "Who tells our stories? Why? How do they influence our thinking?" We also explored the flip side: "Whose stories are not told, and what do we lose because of this?" We read Michael Schaara's *The Killer Angels*, Paul Fleishman's *Bull Run*, and various articles by Garry Wills and others

> *"To perceive, a beholder must create and use his own experience."*
>
> **—John Dewey**

Students can be asked to find images about a unit topic before reading. These can be used in frontloading activities like timelines or floorstorming.

about how Lincoln used the battle and his Gettysburg Address to change the meaning of the war and the meaning of the Constitution, thereby reshaping the future of our nation. The kids used our field trip experiences as a way to think about and make meaning with the texts, and also as a way to understand the influences of particular events on history and politics.

This kind of work is consistent with Tharp and Gallimore's notion (1988) that learners need a concrete experience they can carry forward to their transaction with a text and then use the experience to create a response that constitutes the learning of something new (e.g., considerations of how the meaning of historical events, including current ones, are shaped and used).

Concrete Objects/Precious Objects/Grab Bags

In this technique, the teacher can frontload by providing concrete objects that will be important in a reading or unit of study, and asks students to do a "see, think wonder" (see page 198), noting details they see that might be important, think to make inferences and connections, and wonder to predict what the story might be about. A variation is to provide such objects or pictures of them in a grab bag for small groups of students. The technique can also be used by students before reading as they create or bring in an object significant to them, or that is related to an inquiry— for example, they might bring in an object related to a friendship before a unit on

Before and
During Reading:
Concrete Object/
Precious Object

"What makes a good friend?" This allows students to activate and build background knowledge about friendship as they share stories about their objects.

The technique can also be used during or after a reading as students create a concrete object or precious object in role as a character. The object should signify a value of importance to the character. The technique can be repeated throughout a longer reading to trace how character values are changing and to explore the reasons for this change.

Finally, the technique can be used at the end of a reading or unit to create a symbolic museum of concepts essential to the inquiry theme—for example, a symbolic museum of friendship.

Timelines

Timelines help students to build background and context for reading by providing a situation and template for reading and learning. This template helps them during their reading to identify key details, to summarize, to see patterns of textual details, to read along indices, and to discover complex implied relationships and what these mean to the implied textual meaning. (All of these are required to meet the CCSS for reading.) Clearly, timelines do powerful work for readers, assisting them in using very sophisticated strategies that many readers never master.

So when beginning inquiry units about historical topics like the Holocaust or the Civil Rights movement, I ask my students to create historical timelines as a way of frontloading their reading. Because they often have no background knowledge on these topics, I might also invite in guest speakers, or we might watch a documentary film.

For instance, to begin our civil rights unit, we watch documentaries, like *Eyes on the Prize*, or movies, like *Selma, Lord, Selma*. These experiences provide foundational background, analogous to the Civil War field trip I described below. Without such experiences, students' learning and reading are not as purposeful.

After establishing some personal connections with the Civil Rights movement, I provide students with lists of important concepts and events from the history of civil rights in the United States. Our readings focus on the African-American struggle for civil rights, and my students work in pairs to research two assigned issues unique to each pair. I then give them a class period to examine with other students in the class how the various issues overlap and relate to each other. The next day, they create a class timeline by putting all the class items in order on a roll of butcher paper and decorating it with appropriate visuals.

Feel free to adapt the following timeline guide for your own use.

Timeline Assignment Sheet
African Americans and the Struggle for Civil Rights

You will be assigned a partner and asked to learn about two or three of the important events or movements listed below. You will then work with everyone else in the class to create a comprehensive timeline of the African-American struggle for civil rights.

You and your partner must do the following:

- Identify your chosen/assigned events. (Items that are not chosen in our lottery will be assigned.)

- Identify the dates or periods of the given event or movement.

- Identify the importance (central focus) and consequences of the cited event or movement. Use the Internet, picture books, articles, DVDs, interviews, and any other resource at your disposal.

- Complete a timeline entry, including a summary of the requested information with the name of the event, dates, importance, consequences, and anything else you think is essential for the rest of the class to know. This information will be put on a notecard so it can be pasted onto our timeline.

- Complete an artistic or graphic representation to complement your event entry, such as a symbol, picture, photograph, graph, diagram, or chart. You may use the Internet to download appropriate images, but be sure they specifically fit your timeline entry. Be prepared to justify the visual you decide to use by explaining how it exemplifies something essential about your entry.

- Finally, you will put your entries together with those of your classmates to create a chronologically correct timeline. Each pair will read through all the entries on the timeline and create a minimum of three important connections between entries which will be highlighted through cross-links, call-outs, or labels to help anyone reading the timeline to see the important relationships and themes between events and ideas.

continued on next page

Events and movements that must be included in our class timeline:

- Dred Scott decision (Scott v. Sandford)

- Abolitionist movement/ William Lloyd Garrison and sons

- John Brown at Harper's Ferry

- Lincoln's election

- Phyllis Wheatley (please read Lasky's picture book *A Voice of Her Own*)

- Nat Turner's slave revolt

- Civil War (The War Between the States)

- Battle of Antietam/Emancipation Proclamation

- *The Autobiography of Malcolm X*/ Black nationalist movement

- Sit-in movement (e.g., Greensboro, NC lunch counter campaign)

- 24th Amendment

- Declaration of Independence

- Constitution of the United States

- Slave importation ban

- Brown v. Board of Education

- Assassination of Lincoln

- Breaking the color barrier in major professional sports

- First black regiment in Union Army, 1862 (cf., the movie or book *Glory*)

- Ben Franklin's formal abolition proposal, 1790

- Adoption of The Bill of Rights

- First slaves brought to America

- Plessy v. Ferguson/separate-but-equal legislation

- Race riots in Newark and Watts

- Martin Luther King, Jr., life and assassination

- The black power salute at the Olympics

- March on Washington/"I Have a Dream" speech

- Chicago Democratic Convention, 1968

- Jim Crow Laws/segregation

- Publication of *Uncle Tom's Cabin*

- Underground Railroad

- Rosa Parks/Montgomery Bus Boycott

- Assassination of Malcolm X

- Rodney King trial

- Selma Freedom March/Freedom Riders

- Extra Credit: any other issue, personality, or movement that should be on this timeline that you find out about

Timeline Follow-Up Activity

With your partner, please demonstrate your understanding of one of the following questions or issues and your opinions regarding it. Use the timeline as your information source for answering and justifying your response to the chosen question. You may present your response in a radio interview, a play, a video newscast, a collage, a piece of artwork, a newspaper, a hypermedia stack, or another format you choose.

- What five events, institutions, individuals, groups, or forces were—or are—the biggest obstacles to achieving civil rights and why is this so?

- What are the most important steps to achieving success in the pursuit of acquiring or preserving civil rights?

- Who were the most influential reformers in the arena of civil rights and why do you think so?

- To what degree have we achieved civil rights in this country and across the world? What still needs to be done to both increase and preserve civil rights? Why do you hold these opinions?

Single-Text Timeline

Timelines can also be created and used throughout the reading of a single text to place-hold what has been experienced and learned. A completed timeline helps students to trace patterns and to see complex implied relationships that occur throughout the text. Teacher Patti Baldwin, for example, has her students create a map timeline of the Oregon Trail as they read Francis Parkman's book on the topic, or a timeline of the events that occur along the Mississippi River as they read Mark Twain's *Adventures of Huckleberry Finn*. Students post significant events in the appropriate places on the timeline and add pictures of these events and descriptions of their meaning. Patti then asks them to go back and visually depict the connections between the events. For example, students can show how Tom and Huck's upbringing informs their treatment of Jim and can help them predict what might have happened in sections of the journey that are not described in the book.

Character/Idea Timeline

Timelines can also be used to tell the personal histories of characters, authors, historical figures, or even ideas and movements. Various characters can be displayed on the same timeline to show how their lives differed or were parallel in certain ways. I recently created a character timeline that showed events in the lives of Thomas Jefferson and John Adams. It clearly displayed how the lives and concerns of these two men intersected at times and were removed from each other at other times. My class could have easily added Benjamin Franklin, James Madison, and other major figures to this character timeline, since these figures were engaged with many of the same issues surrounding the Revolutionary War and the founding of our country.

Brainstorming

The easiest and most common form of frontloading is simple brainstorming. It is another technique that helps students to move from accessing available life images to creating and internalizing image-making capacities. Brainstorming is frequently used to introduce units because it is an effective way of stimulating, sharing, and recording the class's combined background knowledge about a topic. And scaffolding results when the class shares and records the vocabulary they know, associated ideas, related questions, and their own personal stories. Research on brainstorming does indicate that students should brainstorm individually before brainstorming in a group to maximize the generation of ideas. Different methods of brainstorming include the following.

Popcorn/Listing

This is a simple activity: Just ask students to write down, then voice ideas that come to mind—to spout them out like popping popcorn. Have one student list the ideas on the board. The idea is not for students to self-edit but to call out any and every idea.

K-W-L-(H)

A popular way of organizing brainstorming is K-W-L (Ogle, 1983). First, have students list what they know (K). Since the group knows more than any individual, all group members are scaffolded to increased understanding. (Also, if someone "knows" something that is in fact incorrect, that misconception is likely to be corrected as all students will be alerted to pay attention to this as they read.) Then ask students to write a list of questions about the topic to which they want to know the answers (W). Purposes for reading are therefore set and shared by the group. Students are alerted to the interests and needs of others and are more likely to share answers or interesting information. As students read and learn, have them list what they are learning in a final column (L). If they have developed a strong interest and/or have a desire to create a social action project—such as a documentary of what they have learned—they will list information they did not initially ask about as it comes up. Further, students can brainstorm how (H) to learn about the questions that have come up.

Floorstorming

For this activity, collect various images or visual displays related to the text or unit that is going to be studied. The displays could include any or all of the following:

- A simple montage portraying elements, ideas, or characters
- A picture map (see page 178)
- A tableau (see page 155)
- The start of a timeline
- A family tree showing relationships or ideas
- Objects and artifacts that will be studied, or that will be important to the upcoming study
- Any other visual that requires students to make inferences, guess at relationships, and pool knowledge about items related to the future topic

Place the images on the floor (hence the name) for a small group to work with. (For a bigger class, the different displays you create for groups to use can be similar or quite different.) Prompt the groups to respond to the images in specific ways; give directions that focus attention on the images and encourage students to brainstorm from them. For example, before my class read the Inuit folktale "The Fast Runner," I provided a montage of an igloo, a broken spear, a kayak, two men fighting, a sealskin coat, a caribou, a man clothed only in a loincloth, a map of Alaska with two distant points highlighted, a summer village, three men chasing another man who is unclothed, and a judge's gavel. I then provided the following prompts:

- Look carefully at the images.
- Describe what you see and what you know about these kinds of places and people. Look at the relationships between the characters, and between the characters and the setting, based on their placements and attitudes towards each other.
- Infer what their relationships might be.
- Look at the whole display, and note what specific details have in common with each other.
- Consider what the topic of the text we will read might be.
- Share what you know about this topic.
- Tell your group what you know and are thinking.
- Draw in or add other details that you know about the topic, places, and people that you think will help you read the story.

Students' responses to floorstorming displays will be scaffolded by the images, which stimulate and support their contributions. Have them record their responses by adding pictures to the displays or by assigning a scribe to record responses in writing.

Webbing From a Picture or Object

As with any of these activities, adaptations and variations abound. For example, when floorstorming, you might ask each student in a group to choose the picture they know the most about and to draw a web of associations around that picture. Students could then help each other to add to each web.

Wheels/Clusters

In this activity, give groups of students different subtopics of a theme to brainstorm, then combine the results into a class cluster or wheel of knowledge. For example, when my daughter's fourth-grade teacher began a unit on the environment, she had groups brainstorm aspects of the environment that affect the quality of human life. She asked small groups to brainstorm everything they could think of regarding how a selected topic— oceans, forests, air, soil, food sources, animal life, geography, climate—might affect how we live, behave, eat, think, and work. Each group made a montage, picture map, collage, or other visual display showing their background knowledge about their topic. The class then created a brainstorming wheel or cluster summarizing their combined background knowledge by putting together all the groups' visualizations. Before combining their finished products, students could walk around to visit other groups' representations and ask questions, make suggestions, and add information.

Self-Text-World Triptych

This triptych activity reinforces the essential insight that to read successfully, we must connect our personal knowledge to the text (self-text connections), bring world knowledge to the text (world-text connections), and bring knowledge from other texts and reading to bear (text-text connections), and vice versa. As good readers learn, they connect their reading back to the world, the self, and to other texts. To make self-text-world triptychs, students divide a posterboard into three equal panels. Prompt them to visualize a topic or an issue related to the reading that comes from their own personal experience. Ask them to create a drawing, collage, or other visualization to illustrate this experience and glue it to the first panel. For the second panel, ask students to draw on their knowledge of history or current events to illustrate connections between the text's topic and the world. This step helps students to identify the larger context for comprehending the text as well as a relevant purpose for doing so. And for the third panel, ask students to

Fiona's self-text-world triptych for Alden Carter's *Bull Catcher* helped her access various resources before and while she read.

create a collage including what they have learned from other, similar texts they are familiar with that might be of use to them. This activity can also be used after a reading to demonstrate what has been learned from a text about oneself, the world, and reading particular kinds of texts.

Using Objects, Artifacts, Photographs, Scrapbooks

The more interesting, intense, and concrete the experiences accessed or built through frontloading, the better for the reader. For this reason, using objects and photographs related to a text (particularly if they are provocatively issue-oriented) helps students to build up background knowledge, images, and interests for use while reading. Teacher Mandie Victor uses this idea in a variety of ways:

Photo Galleries

Before reading texts about D-Day with her middle schoolers, Mandie sets up electronic photo galleries on her students' computers (all seventh graders in Maine currently have laptops due to the Maine Laptop Initiative). These galleries contain photos of D-Day preparations, the voyage across the channel, the beachhead, the parachuting, French families, and more. Mandie asks her students to view the photos and make inferences. She prompts them with questions such as *When were these photos taken? Who are the people in the photos? What is the situation? What different groups of people are involved? What are the goals of each group?* As they do this activity, students practice the important strategy of inferring from visual cues and also help each other build background knowledge.

Video Clips

Rather than using a whole documentary, Mandie uses short video clips to create interest and build background about a text. For instance, before her D-Day unit, her students watch short clips from a PBS documentary about the invasion. She prompts them to ask what the clips have in common and what progression or relationship there might be between clips. As they watch particular scenes, she also asks students to imagine themselves in the role of a combat soldier, an American soldier at a desk job, a dead soldier, a family member back home, a commanding general, a French citizen, or a German soldier. She then asks students to provide an in-role commentary or reflection about the scene from their character's perspective. Students share their responses to learn about the various perspectives involved in this conflict.

Scrapbooks

To build background knowledge and a basis for later responses, Mandie often creates scrapbooks of important background information with her students before pursuing a unit topic, such as Living Through the Depression. The scrapbooks can be created on paper or simply used in electronic format. Parents, grandparents, and community members from a retirement home near school can all help with this project. Students then take over this process, adding to the scrapbooks as they read, or creating one on their own about a character, issue, or theme. In fact, all good front-loading activities should serve students throughout a reading, whether implicitly as a source of information that guides them or explicitly as a template, such as a scrapbook they add to throughout a reading, to visibly show the knowledge they are accruing and constructing.

Camera Crew

To show connections between lived experience and text, teacher Brooke Merow sends middle school students out as digital camera crews on scavenger hunts as units are introduced. She might assign them to find a photo that represents an idea or issue, such as something that represents friendship, inequality, or power relationships. Or she might ask them to take a photo that captures a strategic convention—irony, symbolism, humor, a strong mood or attitude—or even a meaning-making device, such as a repeating shape, different kinds of lines, an interruption, or something colorful. Brooke uses these photos as a way to introduce kids to ideas or techniques in the text they are about to read. Kids discuss how certain devices, like color in a photograph, can draw attention to an object or idea. This leads to a discussion of the ways in which authors draw attention to certain objects or ideas. The concrete experience of taking photographs helps students to see connections between their environment and the text, and to use their own photographs as a way of extending their existing thinking in order to understand more sophisticated and abstract uses of these ideas.

Video Clubs/Art Clubs/Photo Clubs

I often run clubs during lunch, a free period, or even after school. These kinds of clubs take little work; you only have to provide a DVD player and projector as well as appropriate media about the topic being studied. Or you can provide art or photo books from the era or about the issue. Just by flipping through books about and magazines from a particular era, kids pick up lots of information and images that motivate their reading. For example, during a study of the Great Depression, I made available several short videos about life at that time, books of WPA photographs, old *Life* magazines, and Cynthia Rylant's book *Something Permanent*, which pairs her original poems with WPA photographs. Some kids were inspired to write their own poems to photographs, others to read more fully about photographer Dorothea Lange. They often made connections between our reading and the visual images I exposed them to.

Text-Picture Matching

There are a variety of ways to have students match texts and visuals to support the initial phases of comprehension. One way is to provide them with visuals before reading, discuss them, and then ask students to match these visuals to scenes or ideas as they read. The visuals might be photos, picture books, videos, and so on. A variation on this is to have students transform, critique, adapt, or add to the provided illustrations in a text. These basic text-picture matching activities can be extended beyond the frontloading phase and done during reading. For example, you might have students seek out or create illustrations in response to their reading, or ask them to write based on an image from the text. All of these methods assist students in seeing the connection between the words and constructions that make up text and the visual meanings these should prompt in the reader's mind. Great models of the results of these techniques are provided in Douglas Florian's poetry books *Laugheteria*, *Mammalabilia*, and *Insectlopedia*.

Anchor Standards for Writing, 1, 2

Studying Ads and Text Structures

To use advertisements in teaching argument and other text structures, gather various advertisements from popular magazines and ask students to look at the shape of the visual details and text, and of the patterns and shapes that are created through objects and layout design. Ask them to identify different structures, such as compare-contrast, definition, classification, and ironic monologue. Then have them search through magazines to find other examples of these text structures. Study them together, and ask students how different purposes are served through different structures, how we can notice particular structures, and what the structures ask us to do as readers. Ask students to identify the following elements of an ad.

> **The data/evidence:** What makes you say so? These are specific details that answer the questions (i.e., make this claim).

The warrants: How do you know that the data supports the claim? Warrants explain evidence. (This is typically implied, as advertisements are almost always unwarranted assertions that do not explain how the evidence is connected to the claim.)

The backing: How do you know whether the warrant can be believed? (Backing is rarely provided in ads.)

Reservations: Why should you hesitate or question? Why might the claim not be true? (Reservations are also rarely provided in ads, but the reader should certainly actively articulate these.)

By studying ads together, your class can identify the elements of argument that are present or missing. My middle school students often bring in ads and complain that they show unwarranted assertions!

Reading Pictures

A variety of techniques can help students to study paintings, drawings, photographs, and other artwork to make analogies between what they are doing as viewers or "picture readers" and what they must do as readers of written text. This is a great way of frontloading readers with knowledge of concepts, since you can match the content of the artwork to that of a text. It can also frontload readers with knowledge of procedures, since artists and authors use analogous techniques for communicating meaning, such as comparison, mood, and irony.

I call on the art teacher and librarian in my school to access works of art. I show these various works of art on the computer or slides and then ask students to do any of the following:

List everything you see in the picture. I ask them: What was your eye drawn to first? How did the artist draw your attention to this? What are the primary and secondary details? How do they work together? With all of these questions, it is important to connect looking at the artwork to the more complex and abstract issue of reading print. For example, point out and explore how authors draw our attention to certain cues they expect us to notice and make meaning of, and that authors link details into patterns to create meaning.

Identify what shapes and patterns are expressed in the picture. I ask students: How are the details arranged in patterns? Pictures, just like texts, have underlying structures. If we know what the structure is, we can know better how to read the image or the text. Explore how to see patterns in a text by paying attention to transition words, how to see compare and contrast details, and how to see cause and effect.

Find the detail that is most salient or powerful to you. I ask: What in the painter's technique or in your experience made this detail stand out? Point out that authors also use various techniques to make words or phrases stand out. (A great text to use to teach this kind of highlighting is *Someplace Special*, a picture book about civil rights illustrated by Jerry Pinckney.)

Study this picture and the relationship between objects and/or people. I ask: What's the story? What has already happened? What will happen? What is the relationship between the objects, ideas, people? What is the feeling or emotional content of the relationship? (Renoir's "La Loge" or Munch's "The Scream" are great for helping students to infer answers to these questions.) Discuss how authors also leave gaps for readers to fill in.

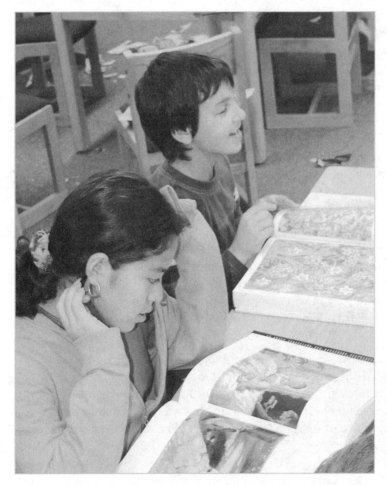

Students study how artists use various techniques to communicate character, movement, mood, or an idea.

Compare the relationship in the picture to a relationship in their reading.
I might compare Mary Cassatt's "Mother Sewing" to the relationship of the uncle and nephew in the picture book *Uncle Jed's Barber Shop*, or to that of Hester and Pearl in *The Scarlet Letter*. Then I ask students: How do the artist and author display facts and feelings about the relationship? What do we learn from this about what we must attend to?

Look at certain pictures and examine a specific feature or technique.
I ask: What different techniques were used? What effects did each technique have on you? Different authors use different styles and techniques to communicate various elements, such as mood or character. Ask students to jot down all the physical descriptions of a character provided by an author and to consider how they highlight particular details, or to consider whether they use any kind of repetition to reveal character attributes.

Look at different works by the same artist, or treatments of the same theme by different artists. I ask: What is similar or different? What differing meanings are communicated through different treatments?

Understanding Perspective

Anchor Standard for Reading, 6
Anchor Standard for Writing, 4

To teach the power of perspective and point of view, art teacher Marilyne Schottenfeld reads a passage from *Stuart Little* as students follow along. From Chapter 8, she reads aloud about Stuart's mother (a human being) mistakenly shutting Stuart (a mouse) in the refrigerator. Thirty minutes later she finds him there, struggling to keep warm on the butter plate. Marilyne then asks students to create two illustrations to show what Stuart saw when Mrs. Little opened up the refrigerator door and what Mrs. Little saw when she looked inside the refrigerator. She has students fold their drawing paper in half and lightly sketch their ideas with pencil. Marilyne prompts them to consider the expression each character would have at the moment they see each other.

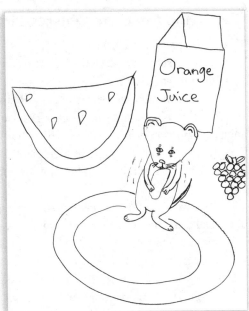

A student sketch of what Stuart's mother sees when she opens the refrigerator door.

Students draw over their sketches with black pens, then share and discuss them in groups, comparing what details from their lives and from the text helped them create their pictures. Marilyne has found that this kind of work, before or near the beginning of a reading, "... gets kids not only to the ballpark, but actually into the game. Once they've made the first couple of plays, they need much less help to keep going."

Marrying Poetry With Abstract Art

Marilyne likes to invite her students to study how abstract art conveys meaning. After discussing a few works of art together, she asks them to select a favorite poem. They then choose a medium that they think would best convey the mood and ideas of the poem. Marilyne asks them to incorporate some actual lines from the poem into the art. They may do this by writing directly on their artwork, or they may choose to glue lines from copies on to their artwork. Or they can use other art supplies to blend the words into their composition, so they look like they belong to the abstract piece. Students then share and explain how their artwork captures their vision of what the text means.

A natural follow-up is to have students find a piece of art and then to write a description of it, a commentary, or a poem that "paints the picture in words" or captures the feeling and emotion of the art. Marilyne finds this a great way to frontload kids through writer's block: "They can't say they don't have anything to write about, and our discussions of art and writing have shown them what things they need to notice and how to make meaning of these cues."

Classifying Concrete Objects/Pictures

Teacher Gerrie Netko begins many of her elementary units with a classification game in which she asks students to sort pictures or objects about the upcoming unit into different groups. (This can be combined with floorstorming.) I observed her introducing a unit on the characteristics of life with just such an activity. She provided students with photographs of various organisms and objects, such as rocks, amoebas, animals, stuffed animals, and fossils of extinct creatures like trilobites and dinosaurs. She first asked students to place each picture into the categories "living" or "nonliving." They quickly realized that to refine the sorting process, they needed additional categories, such as "extinct."

After discussing the life characteristics implied by each class of photos and individual examples, Gerrie asked students to define what makes something animate or inanimate, and then pushed them to begin to define characteristics of life by looking for shared traits and by comparing the pictures they had classified as living to those in the other groups. On the heels of this, she asked students to do a "sketch to stretch" activity. She read a short essay entitled "What is Life?" and asked students to draw images of what they saw in their minds as she read. When done, she asked small groups to create a picture that would summarize the overall point of the essay about what constituted life and what was not living.

Gerrie told me that most students captured only one main idea from the text and did not represent the concept of a life span as a sequence of birth, growth, maturity, maintenance, aging, and death as described in the essay. This gave her valuable information as she planned how to teach the unit on cell biology and the biology of organisms that followed this frontloading activity.

Such an activity can lead to work on writing extended definitions, a very important type of writing in scientific classification. This kind of writing is also the basis for most laws and legal interpretations, and is important in ethics, medicine, and math.

Resources

Below are some books to give students as models for illustrating poems and songs.

Double Vision by Michael and Peter Benton matches masterworks of art with poems written about them.

Something Permanent by Cynthia Rylant matches WPA photos to Rylant's original poems.

Talking to the Sun by Kenneth Koch and Kate Farrell is a compendium of poems and collages.

I, Too, Sing America: Three Centuries of African American Poetry by Catherine Clinton, contains illustrated poems.

Love to Langston by Tony Medina, a poetic picture biography.

Cool Melons Turn to Frogs: The Life and Poems of Issa by Matthew Gollub juxtaposes biography poems and illustrations in an interesting manner.

Hoofbeats, Claws & Rippled Fins, edited by Lee Bennett Hopkins.

Creature. More poems selected by Lee Bennett Hopkins.

Earth Always Endures by Neil Philip matches photos to poetry by Native Americans.

Knock at a Star; A Child's Introduction to Poetry by X. J. Kennedy and Dorothy Kennedy.

This Land is Your Land by Woody Guthrie. Artist Karen Jakobsen uses oil landscapes of iconic American images to amplify the story told in this this musical composition.

Grab Bags

Elementary school teacher Phyllis Bull uses a technique she calls "grab bag" to provide students with the visuals they need to approach a story. She puts photos, found objects, maps, and other visual connections to a text in a bag, and gives one bag to each student as a resource to "take on your reading journey!" After reading, students are asked to create their own grab bags. Phyllis's directions for students to create their own grab bags are as follows:

- Identify story facts, such as the major characters, settings, and conflicts, as well as personal ideas and responses such as the issues, concerns, "ah-has," and themes that you discover as you read.

- Collect objects, pictures, and drawings that represent ideas from the text that are most important for you to remember. (Students may choose to focus on text facts, ideas and responses, or both, depending on their needs and classroom purposes.)

- Label each item in the bag to explain its connection to your reading of the text.

- Put the title, author, and a picture representation of the text topic and main idea or theme of the text on the bag. Decorate the bag to illustrate these ideas.

- Try to have at least six items in your grab bag. Share your bag with your literature circle group. Be prepared to explain what your objects mean to you as a reader of the text.

Phyllis provided me with this example of how one might create a grab bag: "For my reading of *Roll of Thunder, Hear My Cry*, I might decide that the book is about the fight for equality. So I might choose a photo of a potholed dirt road to help me symbolize the feeling of the children as they walked to school and were splashed by the whites-only school bus. I might make a picture of a school bus with a broken axle. This "victory" over the school bus represents their fight to be equal. I might also put in a picture of a Cadillac to show how Uncle Hammer tried to show he was as good as the white people, of a weightlifter to show how Mr. Morrison used physical strength to protect his rights, of a brain to show how Papa used strategy and smarts to help preserve their rights. I could put in a piece of cotton and a match to show how Papa saved TJ from being lynched. Maybe a picture of a white lawyer to show how Mr. Jamison tried to help. Or a simple piece of red paper to signify the anger they all had to overcome, if they were to survive."

"Artworking" One's Way to Understanding

So many times I have witnessed students laughing and sharing as they study pictures or talk together about their drawings, artworks, or other visual creations. I have seen students who were clearly resistant and unenthusiastic about beginning a new unit working excitedly to infer the similarities among several pictures. They could figure out through the pictures what our unit theme was and often discovered that they could connect the unit to prior knowledge and interests.

I remember Jamaal, at the end of an inquiry unit on the question "Who were the greatest figures in the Civil War?" telling me: "Hey, the drawing was absolutely key, you know? If I hadn't done those drawings at the start, and made the scarves for the different characters, and talked about it, I wouldn't have understood the big conflicts and issues... what was at stake. Then it was easier to read the stuff and to talk about it and to see what was important about learning all this and how I was connected to it. I could see how we are all still connected to it, politically and all. I kind of drew and 'artworked' my way into being able to understand."

Jamaal is right on. All of these frontloading activities invoke Vygotsky's notion of "thought on the way inwards"—students acting, drawing, talking, and visualizing their way from concrete images and hands-on visual strategies to more abstract meanings and complex comprehension processes. That's why frontloading is so key— it helps us achieve our ultimate goals of achieving understanding and use through the activation and building of conceptual background and the development of profound procedures of reading and problem solving!

CHAPTER 7

TIME AFTER TIME

Sequencing Strategies That Help Students Meet the Next Reading Challenge

It was one week into our civil rights unit, framed by the essential question "What are my civil rights and how can I best protect them?" The wording of our essential question meant that we would be writing a problem-solution paper at the end of the unit. My students knew that we had to gather data about civil rights, threats to civil rights, and potential responses to these threats so we would have the stuff to write about. They also knew that we needed to learn about how to define civil rights, threats, and how to offer solutions. They knew that this kind of composing embedded definitions into an argument. They knew we would meet several CCSS standards for reading and writing expository and argument texts throughout our unit work, and they knew how this would be important in their lives inside and outside of school.

We began the unit, of course, with frontloading: by brainstorming all the ways that school violated our civil rights. (Have you ever met an eighth grader who doesn't think his civil rights are being violated all the time?) It took us about three minutes to fill up the whiteboard. I then asked the students to choose the most important violations of civil rights that they thought we could do something about, and this was discussed. We posted anchor charts around the classroom with tentative definitions of civil rights, lists of civil rights, lists of threats to civil rights, and lists of protections or responses to threats. These lists would be revised throughout the unit as we read and learned.

Later in that first week, we listened to civil rights songs and read protest poetry—looking for implied meanings and practicing our use of QAR "think and search" and "author and me" questions. We then illustrated the poems' implied meanings, watched a video introduction to the Civil Rights movement in America, and interviewed two guests, one Native American and one African American who were active in civil rights for many years. Before the weekend came we had finalized plans to meet in groups to watch various movies about civil rights so we could engage in jigsaw discussions about them early the next week. Then we'd begin to read primary source documents from the civil rights movement and move to reading *Roll of Thunder, Hear My Cry*. We had used the initial frontloading to move into a sequence of activities that built our conceptual background knowledge, helped us practice new strategies (questioning and asking inferential questions), honed our interest, and prepared us for success for more challenging activities later in the sequence.

As we explored in the previous chapter, frontloading is the first instructional move a teacher makes—at the beginning of any new unit or before any new text or reading challenge—toward supporting students' comprehension. It opens the gate for students to achieve a deeper understanding of content, to develop new interests, and to use new reading strategies. This chapter explores how to follow frontloading with instructional sequences that further develop students' reading, composing, and thinking abilities.

The sequences of support may include readings, visualization activities, and other rituals that scaffold students' abilities to higher and higher levels. Later in this chapter, I share some great activities to carry this out, but first I want to place these sequencing strategies in a teaching-learning model that is crucial for you to buy into! When you embark on using any of the visualization strategies, this model will give you the "pegs" to hang them on for sustained, successful instruction.

Sequencing Is Like Good Parenting

My biggest teacher research project ever has been raising my daughters. How my wife and I taught them to read is a good first example of instructional sequencing. We gave our daughters cloth books about the same time they first gummed infant cereal, and we were astounded at how quickly babies can understand concepts of print—turning pages, looking at pictures, anticipating the funny parts, and so on. In time, we involved our girls in many activities that might seem tangential to learning to read, like going to the zoo, planting a garden, and talking about movies. These experiences gave them background experiences and language they could use later in speaking and then reading.

We knew that our daughters would not learn to read in a day, a week, or even a year. We were in for the long haul, establishing a sequence of life and reading experiences that would help them to grow memory by memory and text by text. We knew we would need to keep introducing them to more sophisticated texts when they had the ability, interest, and need for them. We also knew that we had to allow ourselves and them ample time to make reading happen.

My wife and I carried around books and modeled our own reading passions. We read aloud constantly, sometimes acting out scenes. It has become a family joke that I will read a poem aloud whenever we have guests, much to the embarrassment of my kids. As our daughters grew up, we kept upping the ante. Children's picture books were replaced by juvenile picture books, graphic novels, then young adult books and magazines, such as *Sports Illustrated for Kids*. When the girls displayed interest in a specific idea or issue, a certain book, author, or particular kind of text, we provided them with ways to pursue these interests. When appropriate, we provided slightly more challenging texts that built on their existing interests and abilities. I read these texts aloud to them, talking about my reading. Sometimes I even left adult versions of the text-type about the house. This kind of availability is important: Children can't advance unless we make available the next accessible challenge.

My wife and I have done much of this intuitively, in some ways almost haphazardly, as many parents do. We didn't sit at the kitchen table and map out an instructional plan for teaching our kids to read from ages three to eighteen! But here we are, celebrating Fiona's 21st birthday this very month, having celebrated Jazzy's 19th last month. Both are inveterate readers and writers—Jazzy tending more towards fiction and Fiona more towards functional texts. But readers and writers they have become—in many ways despite their schooling. As a teacher, I have come to articulate how this same teaching-learning process between parents and children can—and should—occur in schools. The process I embrace is much like putting the pieces of a giant puzzle together. Students learn to become strong, independent readers when adults like parents and teachers help them add new reading strategies piece by connecting piece. Gradually, a coherent picture of the expert independent reader emerges—revealing the complete repertoire of mastered skills possessed by the highly proficient readers.

Sequencing Takes Time

As simple as it might first seem, assembling a puzzle isn't a speedy endeavor. It requires patience and perseverance, just as both teaching reading and learning to read do. The process calls to mind one of my favorite sayings, which I learned from hearing the Archbishop Desmond Tutu talk about dismantling apartheid and his work with the Truth and Reconciliation Commission in South Africa: "Eat your elephant one bite at a time." As he would add: "That is the only way to eat an elephant!" One step at a time is the only way we can successfully address big challenges.

Sequences are sustained endeavors because all deep learning occurs through repetition over time, as we gradually layer new meanings on top of established ones. For example, in vocabulary instruction (Brown, Collins, & Du Guid, 1989), research shows that the average teenager has learned 17 words a day throughout his life simply by using language. In contrast, studying lists of words and using them in sentences, as we often do in schools, does not build vocabulary. With this kind of studying, definitions are rarely learned in a meaningful way and are quickly forgotten. For example, in learning the word *cap*, a child might first imagine, based on experience, that it means a black woolen hat for the head. Through hearing *cap* repeatedly, the child learns that the word can refer to various kinds of tight-fitting headgear (skullcaps, baseball caps, and so on) as well as to other objects that cover the top of something, such as a polar ice cap. Eventually, the child learns that *cap* can also be a verb that means to top off something, as in "capping spending." Achieving a deep and flexible understanding of any word takes time and requires repeated experience of the word in meaningful contexts.

This kind of naturally occurring "sequence" is sometimes referred to as "tacit instruction." Some researchers (Hillocks et al., 1971; Beach & Appleman, 1984) argue that repeatedly reading a text convention or structure in a kind of informal sequence can help us to know how to read, interpret, and use these conventions. But other research (see, for example, Smith, 1987) shows that explicit sequences of instruction in how to use different text tools and conventions (such as ways to recognize and understand symbols, irony, or inference gaps) lead to more efficient and powerful learning, particularly for students who may not read widely or who struggle with

Sequencing in a Nutshell

Sequencing is all that you do to teach and support students through a significant zone of proximal development. It is modeling at the point of need, moving to mentoring and monitoring as independence grows, and providing whatever support is necessary to complete significant tasks. We sequence instruction to make sure that we are continually raising the bar for students, moving learning from the concrete to the abstract and fostering significant new strategic abilities.

reading. This kind of sequencing work is known as "apprenticing" readers into expert practice.

In any event, some kind of sequence is necessary for us to deeply understand the demands of a particular text—the demands of its vocabulary, ideas, and text conventions—and thus apply appropriate strategies to comprehend it. Taking the time to guide your students through sequences leads to the profound, transferable-to-life learning that rarely occurs in schools because of our headlong push for coverage of information.

Sequencing Is Based on a Learning-Centered Apprenticeship Model

The major idea behind sequencing is that we must apprentice students (Collins, Brown, Newman, 1992) to become more expert at such cognitive skills as those that make up reading. The apprenticeship model is built upon four key elements that are essential to deep learning:

- The **social context** of the students and of the learning. All people learn best in real situations! In fact, current research supports the notion that we cannot learn without a meaningful context where the learning can be used.

- The **treatment of content**, by teacher and student, as a tool—a form of social action that can accomplish things in the real world.

- The **method of the teacher**, who focuses on assisting student strategy-use and gradually releases responsibility for that strategy-use to the student.

- The **sequencing of activities** and materials from the known to the development of new strategic capacities.

Situate It

In all learning-centered models, the sociology of the learning is key. Learning should build from students' interests and abilities and connect to their current social context. Learning should be purposeful and problem-centered because learners need the opportunity to observe, invent, practice, and hone expert strategies in a context of real use. They also need to get feedback within the context in which knowledge is developed and used.

These authentic situations are filled with sensory details that assist learning, and many of these details are visual. For example, the best way for me to learn how to cross-country ski is by skiing down a trail with a teacher. Within that context, I receive feedback from my performance and from my teacher, and use this to adjust my technique. I can quickly discover whether my herringbone technique is good enough to make it up a hill. If it's not, my teacher can offer tips, model techniques and I can immediately see if and how certain adjustments work.

Children thrive when they are given a chance to collaborate.

The context of use is therefore essential to my learning this particular skill. If I only talked about cross-country skiing techniques, or only tried them in my socks on the living room floor, I wouldn't learn to ski. You might laugh at the exaggeration of this example, yet this type of learning, which is divorced from real contexts, is all too typical of what frequently happens in school.

Offer Multiple Contexts

The cognitive research base shows that using skills in multiple contexts during a sequence greatly assists students. In learning to ski, I'd want to try different trails, with hills and different pitches and turns, in order to gradually make things harder. If I can adapt and transfer my technique to different situations, then I have truly learned it. The same is true of reading: Trying out and repeatedly practicing different inferencing skills by using cartoons, photographs, fables, and short stories greatly increases inferencing ability.

Model It

Students also benefit from seeing various models of expertise in use. They need to experience masters (teachers and other experts) and apprentices (other students) engaged in meeting target skills at varying levels of expertise. This provides benchmarks of progress and helps them to identify their own strengths and weaknesses, goals for improvement, and alternative ways of solving the strategic problem at hand. Visuals are excellent for showing and sharing how different students use particular strategies.

Make It Social

Authentic situations are intrinsically motivating. Students tend to improve their skills when they are participating with others—when there is a social reward for advancing their skills. For example, when I could first ski up a hill, and later when I completed my first ski marathon, the thrill at my growing competence was exquisite, and it was enhanced by the applause of my skiing buddies and teammates. Interestingly, I well remember learning to skate-ski twenty years ago. For twenty years, I've practiced my technique on a masters team, Idaho Nordic, and worked on my strength and endurance with my training partners. I've skied over 40 marathons and had a great time doing it. This last year, I placed third in the U.S. Masters Nordic Skate Marathon for my age division. If the medal wasn't already bronze, believe me, I would bronze it! The takeaway: you can only learn to ski by skiing. Or to read by reading. And by getting assistance in meaningful social situations over time that improve authentic performances in real situations.

The Content: A Means to an End, Not an End in Itself!

Curricular content is typically regarded as established sets of information (the *what*), usually packaged in textbooks. This became painfully clear to me when I went to our local school's parent night. Several teachers talked about quizzes, standards, state tests, and the importance of "getting the required information." No one talked about learning how to be a better reader or problem solver, or about achieving deep mathematical or historical understanding. The new CCSS will reframe our priorities and our consideration of teaching processes, and focus on teaching kids how to think like historians, mathematicians, scientists, and the like.

Apply Knowledge

In cognitive apprenticeship, the emphasis is placed on learning strategies that help us do something (the *how*). The *what* is still essential; but there is recognition of the fact that we learn content most deeply by using it to think, problem solve, or argue—by using it to actually accomplish something. Strategies and the content they operate on, and the relationships between them that are created when we solve problems, can all be powerfully taught and modeled through various visualization techniques.

Making Information Useful

Learning-centered teachers believe that "content knowledge" includes the following strategic procedures that make information usable and powerful:

Heuristic strategies: rules of thumb and other intellectual tools and principles that flexibly guide problem solving.

Control strategies: comprehension monitoring, evaluating, decision making, and applying knowledge to real situations.

Learning strategies: strategies to use in finding, acquiring, and integrating new information into our schema.

Text-specific/genre strategies: comprehension strategies required by particular kinds of texts (arguments, satires, classifications, ironic monologues, lyric poetry).

Task-specific strategies: comprehension strategies required by a particular convention or text-code that can occur in any kind of text (e.g., readers must detect cues for symbolism, irony, foreshadowing, inference gaps, and then construct implied meaning).

Sequencing Guides Students to Independence Gradually

Visualization techniques can be powerfully used at each phase of instruction.

Model: Teacher Does/Students Watch

The expert (usually the teacher) carries out the task in a real situation so students can observe the process. Visual models of the completed task, in which the use and "social work" of doing the task are highlighted, may also be provided.

Scaffold: Teacher Does/Students Help

The teacher carries out pieces of the task that students cannot yet manage and asks students to help in ways that they can manage. The teacher provides assistance and prompts.

COACH: Students and Teacher Do Together— Sharing Responsibility

As students gradually assume more responsibility, the teacher helps by prompting and assisting—articulating the knowledge, reasoning, and problem-solving processes of the expert; naming the processes and ideas students are using; and naming or modeling what students are not yet doing but could do next. The teacher names and demonstrates what kids need to do.

PEER COACH: Students Do/Teacher Helps

Students work together. The teacher helps only if and when needed, coaching through feedback, hints, reminders, prompts, and scaffolding.

EXPLORE: Students Do/Teacher Assesses and Helps as Needed

The teacher fades into the background, encouraging student autonomy in problem setting and problem solving. Students independently meet tasks as the teacher assesses and plans future instruction. Students are allowed to set their own questions, frame problems, and pursue their own reading and inquiry.

REFLECT: Students Consider and Name What They Have Learned

Students are assisted with consolidating their learning by comparing their own problem-solving processes with those of experts and other students. Students are helped to set goals for future learning.

In many ways, the learning-centered approach leads to student-centered learning, as kids use what they have learned to pursue their own agendas and do their own work—the goal, I would argue, of all learning.

Sequencing Takes Students From the Known to the New

When you select texts and activities for an instructional sequence, the following principles will help you plan. Your texts and activities should move from:

- the visual and visually supported to the less visual and visually supported.

- the "close to home" (near to student experience) to the "far from home"—from the most accessible to the least accessible; from the students' current abilities to the gaining of new abilities.

- the direct and literal to the indirect, with high inference loads.

- the concrete to the abstract.

- the short to the long.

- the global to the local, and then back again to the global (students begin with an understanding of global purposes— they know why they are learning the strategy and how they will use it immediately and in the future).

- teacher-involved to student-involved.

- similar tasks to more diverse forms of the task.

- performing the task with similar texts to performing it with a variety of texts.

- collaboration to individual.

Theoretical Links

These principles for planning sequencing activities are consistent with schema theory and transactional theories of reading. They are all based on the understanding that learning proceeds from the known to the new and must be grounded in students' current experiences, interests, and abilities.

Sequences Accommodate All Learners

Sequences can accommodate individual differences in interest and achievement, differentiating instructional support across various groups or individuals. This can happen when all students are involved in learning the same strategies for similar purposes, or when they are inquiring into different aspects of the same topic or inquiry theme. For example, different students can be variously:

Working on the same strategy through different texts that are appropriate to their interest and abilities. Some students might work on inferencing with picture books, while others hone their inferencing strategies through short stories or young adult novels.

Working on the same conceptual topic but with different texts or text-types. Some readers may be reading picture books about race relations, like Patricia Polacco's *Pink and Say*, as others read young adult nonfiction, like Walter Dean Myer's *Now Is Your Time*, popular magazine articles, and newspaper clippings about the same topic. And more advanced readers may be reading even longer and more sophisticated treatments, such as Anne Moody's *Coming of Age in Mississippi*.

Working with various levels of support. The teacher can work with some students (Teacher Does/Students Help) while other students work together (Students Do Together/Teacher Helps) as the teacher comes around occasionally to prompt them. Or students might use exit tickets to help shape the next day's work, while others could be in the final phase of the sequence continuum, working through texts in small groups or on their own (Students Do/Teacher Watches). Students can learn with different methods or in different group structures.

In each of the above cases, all students are involved in the common inquiry projects of the class and benefit from each other's work through sharing and reflection. With the current legislated emphasis on assisting all students, and on raising achievement within minority groups and special education populations, such sequencing structures adequately challenge and appropriately support learning for all students in the classroom. Inquiry-based sequences can therefore help you to teach for each student's strongest self and to promote his or her potential in the most powerful ways, while still teaching a unified unit to the class.

CHAPTER 8

SEQUENCES FOR FINDING MAIN IDEAS
Learning to Get to the Gist

In this chapter, I'll demonstrate how to bring all these pedagogical ideas to bear on some useful sequences for teaching reading. Strategies like making simple inferences, as well as seeing complex implied relationships across texts, are both necessary to comprehending main ideas and the themes of complete texts.

Discovering Theme or Main Idea: Connecting the Author's Dots

One of my favorite sequences is designed to teach students how to find main ideas, which is obviously important to the reading of any kind of text in any subject area. To discern main ideas, readers must first identify the topic (the general subject of a text), then they must identify the key details. But these two steps are not

Teasing Out Terms

The "main idea" is also known as the central focus, thematic statement, or authorial generalization.

enough. Expert reading requires readers to understand the relationships between details, and through this understanding to comprehend the main ideas about the topic. The main idea or theme is an idea that goes beyond the text—an idea that can be applied to the world.

Main ideas can be directly stated, which typically happens in informational text and arguments. They can also be simply implied by the patterns of key details, which is usually the case with literature. For readers, the challenge—and the joy—is to connect the dots of these patterns in order to discern what the author is saying about life. For example, to understand what Lois Lowry is saying about the topic of protecting civil rights in *Number the Stars*, we must look at the pattern of what the Danes—and in particular the Johannssens—did to protect their Jewish neighbors during World War II. We must then look at what the Jewish population did to help themselves. And finally, we must consider which actions worked and which did not. Only seeing across the patterns of these details can we understand the point Lowry makes about the topic of protecting civil rights (i.e., that we must work together as an entire community to define and protect these rights).

Identifying main ideas and supporting these with evidence from the text are skills that our national assessments (the NAEPs) continually show only a minority of our graduating seniors actually possess. And the numbers for these higher level skills are decreasing, perhaps as a result of our renewed emphasis on teaching information instead of strategies. On the last NAEPs, published for 12th grade, only six percent of high school seniors were found to possess these proficiencies—a shocking finding. How can students become active citizens of a democracy if they cannot discern and judge the central underlying principles behind texts, such as speeches, proposals, and op-ed pieces? And again, the CCSS *require* that all students learn how to do just this!

Reading for Main Ideas: A Sample Sequence

The type of main idea sequence described here can be used—and, as the statistics suggest, is certainly needed—by all students to improve their skills in identifying and providing evidence of main ideas. With various adaptations, it has been successful with students of all abilities, from elementary school through high school. Here's how it played out in a unit on adolescent health I did recently with middle schoolers. As I planned the unit, I considered two tasks that are essential from the outset:

Setting social context. I first introduce the inquiry question: "What is healthy living?" The class and I then brainstorm sub-questions, such as: "What do we need to be healthy?" What are the biggest health issues facing tweens and teens? I tell students that we will interview several healthcare professionals, do a lot of nonfiction reading, and eventually engage in small-group research about topics that have come up that are of great interest to them. At the end of their small-group inquiry, they will create a multimedia proposal about improving the health conditions of our school or community.

Introducing the content. Through activities and readings, I introduce students to several content topics around our inquiry question, such as nutrition, drugs, exercise, independence and parental relationships, social acceptance, and dealing with pressures. Each activity or reading is issue-oriented, including how additives and certain kinds of food preparation can harm our health, how the misuse or even the sanctioned use of drugs can change body functions and threaten health, how life habits such as video gaming can encourage physical indolence, and other issues of mental and physical health appropriate to the group, since my initial strategic goal is to help the students identify various subtopics of our inquiry theme.

I Do/You Watch

After sharing the inquiry question, I open the unit by providing students with a collage of different kinds of junk food. I reveal one picture at a time and I talk my way through what I see as the similarities and differences between each new picture and the preceding ones. In this way, I can think aloud about how topics are discerned through the common elements between key details. A topic, in fact, is what all the key details hold in common, and it should be expressed as specifically as possible.

I next show students a collage of individual athletes involved in basketball, soccer, tennis, golf, swimming, and running. I ask them to list each key detail—there's a boy playing soccer, a girl hitting a tennis ball, and so on. Finally, I ask them what the topic of the collage is, reminding them that this would be the general subject of the collage. To find this, we need to find the most specific category we can that would include the common elements of each of the key details, since a topic is what every key detail has in common.

I focus on key details. My students typically identify the topic as "sports." When I ask them why it couldn't be "games," they argue that sports and games differ in certain respects. For example, they might suggest that games are played more for fun than for winning, or that they don't require sweating and aerobic activity. I usually can agree with their ideas, but then challenge them to come up with a more specific topic statement. If they don't come up with "competitive sports," I offer it myself.

Some students might disagree with this topic statement because all of the pictures are of individuals. So how can we know that these people are competing with someone else? Together, we examine the details of the pictures—lane lines in the pool, dress jerseys worn by the basketball player and runner, the lights shining on the soccer player—which lead us to infer that every individual pictured is indeed in a competitive situation. Some students might then offer that the topic is "individual performance in competitive sports," since each photo is of an individual and this is a key shared feature. I tell myself and my students, "Now we are getting somewhere!" And I also ask them what the first collage has to do with the second one, so they can see the connections between the different topics that we will study (junk food and exercise are both aspects of adolescent health, our inquiry topic).

I follow with a similar activity. This concept of "classing" or grouping common elements is a prerequisite to reading, writing, and understanding classification and extended definition text structures. So I reinforce the last activity with the Five Guesses Game, for which I give my students a list, revealing the items one at a time: potato chips, Mudpies, nachos, Twinkies, donuts. As each item is revealed, I guess what the topic might be. I make various mistakes and ask the students to correct me. They must explain first how they know I have made a mistake, and then how they know their topic statement is better.

You Do/I Watch

After Reading: Coaching How to Represent Key Details and Main Ideas

After I have modeled the game, I ask students to play it on their own, and I provide help as it is needed. I reveal the list one word at a time. Students write down a guess as to the topic of the list each time a new item is revealed. With each new item, they can revise or confirm their previous guess and explain why. To up the ante, I put one item in the list that doesn't fit; in this instance, that might be a healthy snack in the list of junk food. This requires them not only to identify and explain the topic but also to identify the oddball item (apples) and the basis on which the item does not fit the topic expressed by the other five examples. (In this case, answers could include any of the following: an apple is a healthy food; it is a natural instead of processed product; it is a complex carbohydrate instead of a refined one; it contains natural fructose and does not contain refined sugar or fat.)

The stated object of the game is to guess the topic as soon as possible, but the real object is to understand how the commonality of key details expresses a topic and what makes a group of key details members of an identifiable class.

Next, I get to the central focus, or main idea. Once students have identified the key details and the common topic they share, I can ask them what statement the details seem to make about this topic. I return to the collages and ask them to identify the comment that is made by the connections or pattern across each of the pictures. I tell them that this statement will be the central focus, or its main idea.

In the case of the sports collage, students typically come up with ideas about the importance of effort to athletic endeavor, or how athletes develop the ability to focus and expend effort (all of the photo subjects have facial expressions that show intense concentration and focused effort). In the case of the junk food collage, students typically come up with notions about how good junk food looks but how bad such foods are for you, as each of the pictures presents the junk foods in very attractive ways. This part of the process helps students to understand how key details work together to express the central focus, or deep meaning of the text.

I recap the process we've been through. Throughout the sequence, each time I introduce a new idea, I coach students in what to do and give them some practice. Then I begin to gradually release responsibility to them, allowing them to coach each other (You Do Together/I Help). At the end of the sequence, we articulate the heuristic, or problem-solving script we followed to identify topics and key details, to see the relationships and patterns among the details, and to infer the point made by these relationships. Summarizing this point as a topic-comment (e.g., competitive sports [topic] require concentration [comment]).At this point, we can reflect on how to apply this script in our future reading. When you try this idea with your students, don't hesitate to actually state the learning benefit, and the terms. Tell them that the ability to see the connections among details and how these connections or patterns create meaning is called inferencing, and it is essential to good reading.

Identifying the Main Idea in Visual Texts

After running through introductory sequenced activities such as those described above, my students generally have the terminology and strategies necessary to identify topics, key details, patterns across key details, and implied central focus statements—at least with collages and lists. Then it's time to add something to the sequence, so I make things harder by adding a different, more difficult kind of text, as you'll see below.

Now that students have the basic script down, I start this next sequence of more difficult activities at the You Do Together/I Help phase. I can always move back to I Do/You Help with students who exhibit difficulties. Likewise, as soon as some students show they have met the new challenge, I allow them to move on to independent practice. In this way, I learn from the students what to emphasize, and my teaching is always responsive to their needs, so I can give small-group or individual attention as needed.

Paintings and Parodies

I often center a more challenging sequencing activity on famous paintings and parodies of these paintings, since parodies change salient details to shift the topic and, therefore, the central focus of a painting. This shows kids how changing even one key detail can radically alter the topic (which must accommodate all key details) and the central focus (the statement about the topic, which must consider all the key details). And it demonstrates how attentive a good reader must be.

For example, when I introduce Grant Wood's famous painting "American Gothic," students usually identify the topic of this artwork as "farm life." Occasionally, they think the topic is "married life." I constantly ask students to justify their topic choices, which requires them to justify their thinking in a way most high school seniors cannot do with text. We practice with these visuals and then move to the more implicit meanings in written texts. So to support the topic of farming, my students might cite the farm house, the side of the barn, the pitchfork the man is holding, and the plain work clothes worn by both the man and the woman. To support the topic of marriage, they cite that the picture shows a man and woman standing together in front of a house. The two are placed close to each other in front of a home we can assume they share. The plain churchlike window of the house's second story implies a religious basis for their enterprises. Their expressions are stolid, careworn, and tired, which my students associate with marriage!

Either of these topics works because both can be justified with details from the text. Realizing this conveys to students that different readers might identify different topics for the same text. This means that it's fine for readers to ascribe different central foci to this same artwork even when they're paying close attention to all of the same codes in the text. Interestingly, the central focus statement is similar for either

"American Gothic" by Grant Wood and Richard Hess's parody of American Gothic topic here: "Marriage is tough" or "Farming is a hard go." The evidence is the same for both: the tired and haggard looks of the couple and the plain, worn clothing.

I then show students Richard Hess's parody of "American Gothic," in which he simply adds gas masks to the faces of the man and the woman. My students get a good laugh, and then I ask them how we must revise our notion of the topic based on this new key detail. Prior to the 9/11 terrorist attacks, most of my students identified the new topic as "pollution," though some who lived in farm communities identified the topic as "toxic fertilizers." Post-9/11, my students almost always identify the topic as "bioterrorism." This clearly shows the transactional nature of meaning making: Based on the knowledge and concerns readers bring to bear, a text will address a different topic and make a different point to them. This new point accommodates the codes of the text and the readers' knowledge base, questions, and current needs or interests.

The key details now also include the farm, but the gas masks are more important. The central focus students usually identify is something along the lines of "Air pollution is everywhere, even out in the country" or "None of us is safe from bioterrorism, even those who live in the country." Both farm life and an airborne threat are essential to establishing the central focus statement as this statement must account for the gas masks.

Practice With More Difficult Texts

After you try activities like the one above, which uses pictures, practice the process of identifying a central focus with increasingly difficult texts. First, try using texts with less visual support, then move to texts that are longer and more abstract, and finally to texts with topics further from students' background experience. To start this process of increasing the difficulty, I use combinations of visuals and text—photos with captions, or comics and political cartoons—so that students must look for patterns across the visual and written text. Then I move to short texts like picture books, illustrated poems, non-illustrated poems, and short stories or articles, practicing the same techniques and using the same terminology. I pay attention to the students and how much practice they need. I don't move on to more difficult texts until they understand how to use the process with simpler, concrete, and more visual texts because the concrete experience with visual texts scaffolds their abilities to the point where they can use the same strategies with written texts.

Finding the Central Focus in Poems

After a couple of days, my students and I are reading poems, such as Shel Silverstein's "My Rules," which starts with "If you want to marry me, here's what you'll have to do..." I ask students the topic of the poem. The title and first line give strong clues that the topic is "Rules for marrying somebody." We then identify the key

Engaging kids in sequences of collages, cartoons, and short texts can cover a lot of ground in very little time, giving kids lots of practice with finding main ideas. It also allows you to turn your teaching around on a dime. For example, if I am using a collage that I discover is too conceptually difficult for my kids, I have wasted just three minutes and can get the lesson back on track immediately. But if I try to teach the same processes while teaching a novel, I might waste four weeks before realizing it didn't work. Shorter is better. Repeated use of a strategy with different texts leads to expertise.

details of the poem, which are mostly the rules themselves: "darn my socks," "be still when I talk," "shovel the walk when it is snowing." Some students think it is also key to infer the gender of the speaker, which is not identified. Most kids think the demanding tone sounds like a male, but some think that since males traditionally ask females to marry them, that the speaker must be a female. If the students identify the speaker's gender as being a key detail, then I remind them that this must be reflected in the central focus statement.

The poem lists many rules that must be followed, and concludes with the final line: "Hey! Where are you going?" The poem's details lead to this central focus: "If you set too many rules and demands for marriage, the person you love will leave you." Or, if a student felt the gender was crucial, the central focus might be: "Men should be careful of setting too many rules for their wives, if they want them to be happy." When students can independently apply this process without the support of visuals, a measure of independence has been achieved—the sequence has begun to do its work.

Writing Summaries and Other Extensions

Make no mistake: reading for the central focus, or main idea, is a profound achievement, a key part of a foundational educational competence. And reading for the main idea must be honed with each new kind of text a student learns to read. Whenever you successfully complete a sequence with students, they are ready for a new one. For example, students who can read for a main idea can easily be helped to compose excellent summaries. Writing summaries can be contextualized and applied through various activities, like writing telegrams, creating picture-book summaries, or creating a set of prompts that encourage a complete summary of a particular text type.

One More Time! The Benefits of Repeated Readings

Every impressive research base demonstrates how students of all ages benefit from rereading. In fact, the work of Sulzby (1985) and others in the field of emergent literacy demonstrates that children learn how to read by rereading. Anyone with small children knows this is true: they drive you crazy rereading the same book hundreds of times! Rereading is a form of sequencing, as each reading provides background and competence with which to approach the next reading. Because the child understands the basic meanings, her intellectual resources can then be used to attend to new words, more sophisticated text features, meanings, and more.

Interestingly, in the American schools where I have worked, teachers are often adamantly set against allowing students to read books they have read before. The only explanation I can find is that they believe that teaching is purely purveying information, so if students are familiar with the information in or plot of a text, there is no purpose for rereading it. But if we are dedicated to assisting students with developing transferable strategies of reading, thinking, and problem solving, then rereading is an essential tool of our teaching. It allows students to develop competence with strategies. This practice of rereading is used extensively in the German, Swiss, and English schools where I have worked. Teachers in those schools seem to understand that deep comprehension and strategic knowledge are developed through this process.

Rereading a Poem With Visuals: A Sample Sequence

I recently saw teacher and former Oregon State Reading Association President Peter Thacker use prereading and rereading in a session he conducted at the West Regional IRA meeting. Peter chose a poem that was about one page long and full of images. In fact, any text that is image-rich will work, including a fable or very short story.

Peter started with the strategy of visual prompting. He read the piece aloud, asking us to keep our eyes shut and to "watch the TV screen of our minds" to identify major images. We did not have copies of the poem, so we had to listen carefully. Peter then reread the poem, this time asking us to try to more fully capture the most important images, adding details and specificity to them. On a third rereading, we were told to more fully imagine and flesh out the details of the strongest images. Notice that each reading served as a prereading (or frontloading) for subsequent readings, and by the end we had done a deep study of the poem by focusing on creating visuals.

For the next reading, Peter asked that we draw the strongest image we captured from the poem, adding the words that fed the image on our drawings. The final step involved Peter reading the poem aloud yet again, stopping at any point anyone indicated that he had created an image. That person presented his image to the class at this point, explained why he found the image to be so strong, and then posted it on the wall. As each succeeding image was presented, it was placed in sequence on the wall from left to right. Interestingly, several participants drew images from the same textual prompts, so there were clusters of images at two points in the poem.

These images were placed vertically along the timeline of images we created. When we were done, Peter asked us if any strong images had been left out. He then asked for volunteers to create drawings to fill those in.

As a class, we then did a gallery walk of our images to notice visual themes—images, colors, tones, shapes, implied actions, or ideas that seemed to recur. We also noticed how different people envisioned the same prompts in different ways and explored why this might have happened. Some images were iconic, some abstract, others very true to life; these different images captured different readers' experiences. At this point we were well into discussing the visual images, the poem, and what we were learning from this activity.

We had been supported in seeing the poem, identifying key details, ordering these details, seeing patterns across the details, and inferring the meanings of these patterns. Then we were asked to justify the discerned main ideas with details from the text. Peter helped us turn the poem into a collage that made the poem more accessible, and on which we could operate interpretively, just like the collages I described in my main idea sequences.

The activity was a powerful sequence in itself, but it could also serve as a kind of frontloading for subsequent readings of other poems or texts using similar concepts or requiring similar strategies.

Reading Between and Beyond the Lines With Visuals: A Sample Sequence

Art teacher Marilyne Schottenfeld has developed an excellent short sequence that helps students to see the difference between reading as literal decoding and reading as seeing stated or simple implied relationships (reading line-by-line, bringing accumulated meanings forward); reading as seeing patterns of more complex implied relationships (reading between the lines, filling in implied and missing meanings); and reading as elaboration and connection to concerns outside the text (reading beyond the lines to make text-to-text, text-to-self, and text-to-world connections). Her sequence helps students to develop strategies for reading in these different ways. Expert readers make use of all these kinds of reading simultaneously as they read almost any text. This sequence therefore helps Marilyne's novice readers to get a fuller view of reading expertise in a visually supported way.

It can be used with any text of short or moderate length; she likes to use it with the poem "The Owl and the Pussy-Cat" by Edward Lear.

The Owl and the Pussy Cat

The Owl and the Pussy-cat went to the sea
    In a beautiful pea-green boat,
They took some honey, and plenty of money,
    Wrapped in a five-pound note.
The Owl looked up to the stars above,
    And sang to a small guitar,
"O lovely Pussy! O Pussy, my love,
    What a beautiful Pussy you are,
          You are,
          You are!
What a beautiful Pussy you are!"

Pussy said to the Owl, "You elegant fowl!
    How charmingly sweet you sing!
O let us be married! too long we have tarried:
    But what shall we do for a ring?"
They sailed away, for a year and a day,
    To the land where the Bong-Tree grows
And there in a wood a Piggy-wig stood
    With a ring at the end of his nose,
          His nose,
          His nose,
With a ring at the end of his nose.

"Dear Pig, are you willing to sell for one shilling
    Your ring?" Said the Piggy, "I will."
So they took it away, and were married next day
    By the turkey who lives on the hill.
They dined on mince, and slices of quince,
    Which they ate with a runcible spoon;
And hand in hand, on the edge of the sand,
    They danced by the light of the moon,
          The moon,
          The moon,
They danced by the light of the moon.

—by Edward Lear

Reading/Drawing Line by Line

Marilyne's goals are to use the sequence to help students create initial visualizations and to build metacognitive awareness—to know how they form mental representations as they read. More than that, though, she wants them to become aware of how mental pictures change and build upon each other as the poem's lines unfold and more information is provided. Literary theorists call this "reading along indices." It is the expert strategy of carrying meaning forward through a reading, of constantly accruing and revising meaning as one gains new information and encounters new cues.

Marilyne puts the poem on the overhead and covers up all but the first line of the first stanza. She has her students fold a piece of large white drawing paper into eight boxes. In the first box, she asks them to draw a small pencil sketch that captures the mental picture they create based on information from the first line. She then uncovers the second line and asks students to repeat the procedure. She does this for each line for the first eight lines of the poem. (They do not draw the three-line refrain.)

When finished, students analyze their progression of line drawings to see how each line provided new visual information to add. Students share their renderings and consider how mental pictures differed and developed as new information was provided. They then create a final illustration that combines all or some of the line-by-line pictures into an image that best represents the meaning of the whole stanza. Finally, Marilyne allows students to add color and other pictorial elements, and to share and reflect on similarities and differences.

Reading/Drawing Between the Lines

Marilyne then proceeds to the next activity, which is designed to help students gain awareness of how good readers read between the lines by creating suggested subtextual meanings, bringing their own personal experience into conversation with the text. This is done in order to fill in gaps or extend and complete patterns left by the text. She asks students to reread "The Owl and the Pussy-Cat" and to create an illustration that goes with the explicit text but fleshes out and adds "unmentioned" details to stated meanings. Her prompts might include:

- What kind of boat do you think they took out to sea? Draw an illustration of the pea-green boat as you picture it. Why did you add the details that you did?

- What do you think a "bong-tree" is? Draw an illustration of how you see it and explain why you see it that way.

- What are "mince" and "slices of quince," and what is a "runcible spoon"? Draw an illustration of this place setting at the wedding banquet, including eating utensils and food.

- Draw a scene from the wedding reception and celebration.

- Come up with any other complete picture that is suggested by the text but is not provided or provided fully.

Students complete their visual renderings and compare them with each other's. They consider differences in how they read between the lines and discuss how life experiences, knowledge levels, and text details might account for these differences.

Drawing/Reading Beyond the Lines

The final activity in this sequence is designed to show how readers go beyond the text to elaborate meanings, infer future events or associations, and connect what has been read to new and quite different real-world situations. These processes allow readers to achieve some form of transfer, as they use textual experience to think about events or issues outside the text.

To start creating a new set of textual meanings, Marilyne tells her students that they will create a rendering that explores probabilities and possibilities not discussed in the poem. These should build on the text to continue the story or apply the textual meanings to new situations. Her prompts might include:

- The owl and the pussycat are, of course, two different species. Draw a picture showing their future offspring.

- Owls and pussycats prefer different kinds of abodes. Design a dwelling that would satisfy the needs and desires of both.

- Predict what their future life will be like and draw a scene from that life. What in the poem and in your experience informs this prediction?

- What particular joys and obstacles do you predict for their union? Draw a two-sided tableau that pictures one joy and one obstacle in their life together.

- What kinds of other unlikely relationships and alliances (familial, political, and so on) do you think this poem might also apply to? Create a collage of unlikely relationships or make a flow chart about how such a relationship might begin and develop.

This sequence leads students to see details, connect these details to make various kinds of inferences, and to think about the text as connected to the larger world. Obviously, it helps them to think about the deep thematic meaning of the poem as well.

Writing About Photographs

Students can use photographs or other visuals as inspiration and scaffolding to write a poem, description, or definition. Likewise, they can provide visuals for their own writing and presentations.

The ice skating rink inside the city gates of Old Quebec, the subject of Jasmine's poem, age 8.

Video Club

Video clubs can be used in a sequence to build conceptual knowledge about a unit theme. I have students arrange to meet in self-chosen groups over a weekend and watch a video from among several choices.

For example, for an inquiry unit on "What is success?" students could choose to watch *Finding Forrester*, *Forrest Gump*, *La Bamba*, *Good Will Hunting*, and

Clockers. Younger students might choose *Pocahontas*, *Shrek*, *Aladdin* or other movies that explore various notions of success.

Check out the reference *Videohounds Golden Movie Retriever* for summaries of movies that are classified around curricular themes!

On the next page is a response sheet you can adapt for use with your students.

Video Club Response Sheet

After you have watched the movie together, answer the following questions as a group. Feel free to talk with your parents and other adults as you do so.

Title of movie(s) your group watched:

1. Describe how success is portrayed in your movie—i.e., what messages about the image of success and achieving success are communicated?

2. Is the image of success conveyed by the movie you watched similar or different from the image of success you hold and/or that our society holds?

3. How do the images of success in this movie compare to other cultural images of success such as those in other movies, in songs you know, and on television?

4. Is there something we need to do about the cultural image of success in our society? If so, what can we do about it? How can we overcome or change the cultural image of success in our own lives?

For extra credit:

5. Visit some Internet sites that feature visual images of success, such as humanityquest.com, home.cogeco.ca/~rayser3/literal.htm, or other sites.

6. Find and read poems about success, like "Success" by Edgar Guest, "Still I Rise" by Maya Angelou, "The Road Not Taken" by Robert Frost, "Richard Cory" by E. A. Robinson, or other poems.

7. Comment on what is being communicated about success through the web images or poems.

The Right Teaching Tools

Frontloading and sequencing are the biggest levers in my teaching tool belt. They are the first activities I rely on when I am designing or teaching a unit. They are my most important tools. They pry kids from where they are and get them moving to where they might go next. One year I taught Kris and Stephan, two struggling and reluctant readers. They complained vociferously about our new civil rights unit until, during the frontloading activities, they realized that sports involved profound civil rights issues and that they would be able to read about this, and write about this.

Through their readings about the Negro Leagues, about Jackie Robinson and Hank Aaron, I led Kris and Stephan through sequences that helped them to understand new perspectives, to see patterns and connections, and to make inferences. For example, later in the unit, when they balked at reading Dr. Martin Luther King, Jr.'s "I Have a Dream" speech and "Letter From Birmingham Jail," I told them that they already knew everything they needed to read these texts. To Kris's dumbfounded "Huh?!" I explained that they could use their knowledge of black ballplayers' experiences and their own work on taking new perspectives to understand Dr. King's situation and writing. And, with a little more assistance to both boys, I was right. They each drew a picture of both settings—the mall in front of the Lincoln Memorial and the Birmingham jail cell—along with pictures of what King hoped to transform through the words he spoke and wrote in these places. The boys created picture maps of each text with topic, details, and central focus. More than that, they used these artifacts to discuss the connections between breaking the color barrier in baseball and Dr. King's struggle, and then compared the two King texts in insightful ways. The boys included quotes and pictures of Dr. King in their final video project about breaking the color barrier in sports.

Stephan complained with a smile that I had tricked them: "You taught us what you wanted us to be able to do by letting us read what we wanted to read." I had to admit that he was right because the "trick" he described is exactly how we move kids along the trajectory of actualizing their fullest potential. It's what my teachers did for me back in school, what my colleagues and co-authors and editors have done for me throughout my writing career, and what my masters Nordic ski coach does for me now—layering on the gains of past years to further hone techniques and performance for this year—helping me to get better day by day, activity by activity, performance by performance.

CHAPTER 9

TECHNOLOGY TO PROMOTE VISUALIZING, READING, AND COMPOSING

21st Century Multimedia and Multimodal Literacies

L iteracy historian and classics scholar Jay David Bolter (1991) shows that being literate has always meant the capacity to use a culture's most powerful tools to create and receive meanings. Those tools are now undoubtedly multimodal and digital. If we don't help our students to critically read, compose, and critique in hypermedia contexts, then we can hardly say we are helping them to be literate. Besides, as I've argued here, the use of visuals in any form, including digital media, can promote decoding and a whole range of strategies for comprehending, responding, interpreting, validating, critiquing, elaborating, and much more.

The CCSS recognizes the importance of multimodal and digital literacies, and includes these in the standards for English-Language Arts and literacy for the content areas. The CCSS promotes an integrated model of literacy, so it is useful to think of reading and composing, as well as speaking and listening, as symbiotic and interrelated parts of a larger whole of literate practices.

The CCSS blends inquiry, research, and multimedia into the standards as a whole, both implicitly and explicitly. Multimodality and digital tools play out in standards regarding student research, reading, composing, and presenting. Here are some examples: Anchor standard 7 for reading: Integrate and evaluate content presented in diverse formats and media, including visually and quantitatively, as well as in words. Anchor standard 6 for writing: Use technology, including the Internet, to produce and publish writing and to interact and collaborate with others. Anchor standard 5 for speaking and listening: Make strategic use of digital media and visual displays of data to express information and enhance understanding of presentations.

Neil Postman argues (1990) that "technology" simply means an extension of human capacities for doing important and substantive work. There are innumerable technological applications that can work in this way, supporting student visualization to develop unconstrained strategies. Many of these tools support student informal composing in ways that promote reading strategies, as well as promoting the composing of the formal kinds of narrative, explanatory/informational, or argument texts required by the CCSS.

A caveat—any tool that can be used to extend human capacities can also be misused or become a throwaway that does not extend these capacities. So when choosing a digital tool, make sure that it is introduced at the point of your students' needs, and that it extends their capacities to develop unconstrained strategies and do significant work *in contexts of actual use* as readers and writers, speakers, and listeners.

Again, the number of tools are numerous and ever multiplying. Here are just a few I have used and that the teachers with whom I work have used to great effect. Though platforms quickly evolve, the principles behind these platforms are sure to exist in various forms.

For Frontloading/Floorstorming

Visuals are a fantastic way to frontload units or challenging readings. Frontloading (Wilhelm, et al, 2001) is simply the activation of students' prior background knowledge that can be used as a resource for addressing the task at hand. Frontloading also builds background, sets purposes, and provides structures, scaffolds, and templates for developing and representing new learning. Visuals and photographs are particularly good for frontloading because they are so immediate, understandable, and concrete, providing fodder for personal connections and inferencing.

The best way I know to get images and photographs for frontloading that might take shape through a museum exhibit, walkaround, or floorstorming activity (all explained and explored in this book) is to do a simple Google search. When I recently taught a unit involving the Depression (organized around the essential question: Why do people migrate?), I Googled "images of American Depression" and got over three million hits. The first hit provided 300 WPA photographs that I used to create mosaics for my students to write about, requiring them to activate and develop background knowledge about this time in history and its human effects.

Creating posters and picture mosaics are also a great activity for students as they respond to their reading. Tools for making posters and mosaics can be found on www.bighugelabs.com.

For Vocabulary Development

Anchor Standards for Language, 4–6

The CCSS has three anchor standards related to vocabulary acquisition and use, and we all know how important vocabulary is to reading, composing, understanding, and advanced problem solving. Knowing how to develop vocabulary will be particularly important to students moving through any zone of proximal development, gaining independence as literate beings, and for helping students to meet the text complexity standards set by the CCSS for college, career readiness, or citizenship readiness.

There are plenty of vocabulary resources online. One online graphical dictionary and thesaurus I've used, at the recommendation of Erika Boas, is called visuwords and can be found at www.visuwords.com. A color-coded key is useful to help students make grammar connections as well.

WordSift (www.wordsift.com) is a site that helps students develop vocabulary through visualization of the most frequently used words in a text. Teachers of ELLs and LFS students as well as struggling readers have had good luck with this tool. There's a great introductory video. I really love this site.

Wordle (www.wordle.net) is a self-described "toy" that creates "word clouds" from the repeated vocabulary in particular texts, which can help students to discern topics and motifs from the texts they are writing and composing. Wordles can also be created from brainstormed lists of related words, or words about a particular character, topic, and so on.

Though Wordle was first, even better in my opinion is Tagxedo (tagxedo.com). This site does the same work as Wordle but adds the extra option of being able to create word images. This is great for picture poems, creating concrete poetry, and creating images with and from short expository texts and the like.

Storybird (storybird.com). The Boise State Writing Project technology liaisons Dianne Ruxton and Samantha Mora (English and foreign language teachers) have students develop vocabulary in the context of their inquiry units. Every other day, kids have about ten minutes (bell activity) to complete work on assigned words via group storytelling (one person starts the story using a word, the next person expands on the story using a different word, and so on) or they use Storybird. The students create a class page, pick out a set of pictures as a class, then one by one, students go to a computer and start working on a collaborative story. The first person starts the story using an image to create a theme, and uses a vocabulary word in the story. The next person has to read the previous passages (ensuring coherence) and continues on with the story. If a person disagrees with the use of a previous word, he or she calls the author of the page back to the computer to discuss the meaning until they either edit the page or agree on the correct use of the word.

Of course, Storybird works great for storytelling as well. Sam uses this in her foreign language class to great effect and Dianne has used it for novel/play retelling, concept stories, or personal narratives told from a different perspective.

Quizlet (quizlet.com). Quizlet is a great resource for students who need to bone up on vocabulary. Dianne posts this site on her web page, and over the course of a unit students can review vocabulary words by playing the games, printing out note cards, or just reviewing.

Spelling City (www.spellingcity.com/view-spelling-list.html?listId=4339342). Dianne also uses Spelling City to help her struggling spellers. This is a program aimed at elementary students but still works for her high school kids.

For Visualizing Story Events, Text Details, and Summarizing

Multimodal Standards for Reading, 7, 9
Writing, 4–6, 8

Several teachers I know (including foreign language teachers) have enjoyed having students recreate stories or do retellings by using 3-D storybooks and pop-up books using the Zooburst site: www.zooburst.com.

Alan Levine hosts a wiki that explores multiple ways to tell multimedia stories, and, of course, these techniques all work for retelling and visualizing stories read in class or on one's own: cogdogroo.wikispaces.com/50+Ways.

When digital teaching guru Troy Hicks visited the Boise State Writing Project this past year, he shared several tools I've since found useful for creating retellings, responses, and group conversations around these.

VoiceThread. A VoiceThread is a collaborative multimedia slide show that can feature images, documents, and videos and allows people to navigate slides and leave comments in five ways—using voice (with a mic or telephone), text, audio file, or video (via a webcam). Kids can share a VoiceThread with other students, teachers, parents, or friends for them to record comments, too.

My Storymaker. This was another online storytelling tool Troy introduced, particularly good for young students: www.carnegielibrary.org/kids/mystorymaker/mystorymaker.swf. Troy shared how we can use various digital comics-creation software programs for both comics and manga—for example, Comic Life (plasq.com/comiclife)—that provide students with templates, images, icons, and fonts for creating comics. Students can use this software to create their own comic book versions of texts they are reading, requiring them to translate the text into a more visual form. I have found this particularly helpful with ELLs, LFS students, and struggling students. (For instruction using comics to teach literary elements and genres, see Smith and Wilhelm, 2010.)

Toondoo is another site for creating cartoons that Erika Boas likes to use. Erika also has students create visual retellings of stories, novels, and other texts by using images found on the Internet. She also encourages them to upload their own photos so that they can make self-to-text or text-to-text connections to the retold text.

As one example, students use Photostory to illustrate poems they have chosen, setting lines of the poetry to music and images. These can be made into PowerPoint presentations. Students can then describe what images are inspired directly by the poem, and which involve self-to-text, text-to-text, or text-to-world connections.

Students can obviously use such tools to create their own original narratives, or their own visual supports for learning or teaching others. I've never seen a concept, strategy, or genre that could not be introduced and taught through comics. Involving the students in creating comics to develop, display, and teach others what they are learning conceptually, procedurally, and in terms of text structure and meaning segue beautifully with the CCSS and is highly motivating to students, giving them immediate and visible signs of accomplishment that are performance based and creative instead of just recall (Smith and Wilhelm, 2010).

Writing original narratives through or with visuals has other benefits as well. In telling narratives in any form, students are dramatizing their responses, ideas, and judgments about experiences or people. Barbara Kamler (2001) argues that narratives encourage students to explore, remake, reframe, relocate, and come to terms with tensions in their lives: "The stories we tell provide the frameworks through which we act. Stories are interpretive resources for dealing with the everyday world and for taking ourselves up within the cultural storylines available to us" (p. 21).

For Multimodal Composing

Another set of literacy tools involves creating and collecting visuals associated with a particular topic, theme, or issue for use in a multimodal essay or blog post, or to create a mural, collage, scrapbook, or online slideshow. Students can easily access digital images on Flickr and Google Images or videos on YouTube based on topic searches. These can be posted on a classroom wiki or other "museum-like" collections about a certain topic. Students can also make original contributions to such collections by finding or creating their own images.

Students can further use these digital images or videos to engage in critical inquiry about media representations of race, class, and gender identities. In a unit on identity ("What makes me me?") I used an idea from my colleague Rick Beach and had students display separate images of their faces and then morph them into different composite images. This led students to reflect on the similarities and differences in their appearance, as well as the roles of difference, relationships, and appearance in identity and identity construction.

Here's a multimodal composing idea that I've had great success using with everyone from National Writing Project teachers to elementary students. Students select a theme song that expresses something about their identity, or beliefs. They share it with the class or with a learning group. They can explain how the song expresses an aspect of identity, or have the group guess how it does. Students can then do the same project using a different role, selecting a theme song for a character or author. Sometimes students enjoy creating whole CDs or song sequences that tell a story that expresses character or aspects of identity, either for themselves or for a character. Song lyrics can be found on songlyrics.com and other sites. Students doing such projects also enjoy designing their own CD covers. Sometimes you will have students who compose their own music. My daughter Fiona produced her own CD of original music and a beautiful CD cover that she felt expressed her personality and

Students can design CD covers for their own CDs, mixes, or for theme songs about characters from their reading.

captured the themes of her music. She then posted her music for sale on CDbaby.com under her stage name of "Fiona Luray."

Likewise, Voicethread can be used for multimodal storytelling. Here's one of Dianne Ruxton's on *The Catcher in the Rye*: voicethread.com/book.swf?b=69839.

Xtranormal (www.xtranormal.com). This is a great format where students and teachers can type in the text, choose their characters and setting, and then apply the text. Students can do this for research projects. For example, one student did this during a unit on Nuclear Warfare: www.xtranormal.com/watch/6594995/nuclear-warfare.

Photo Peach. This great tool can be used to combine music, text, and images to tell a story. Here's one on Roald Dahl: photopeach.com/album/12r1fdg?ref=est.

Museum Box. Another good tool is Museum Box. It can be a bit tedious to create an account as a user, but once that's done, it allows the user to create a three-dimensional box integrating/embedding images, text, and video. Boise State Writing Project fellow Bob Foster created a great one for *Animal Farm* during one of our technology institutes at: museumbox.e2bn.org/creator/viewer/show/93316

Photostory. Finally, Photostory allows students to put together vocal recordings, images, and text to tell a story. Teacher Maura Brantley's example of a poem can be found here: www.youtube.com/watch?v=A7VXuYMj170&feature=player_embedded.

For Murals and Mapping

Murals and mapping portray and represent places and spaces, as well as processes, textual unfolding, and development. Another useful tool for visually representing ideas and perceptions of places/spaces is "mindmapping." Students can use mindmapping to develop topics and ideas and then make visual connections between topics and subtopics to help them perceive the logical relationships between topics and subtopics and details. Rachel's students have used this online tool to create and embed mindmaps in larger multimodal compositions: www.edrawsoft.com/freemind.php.

When composing expository texts such as definitions, comparison-contrasts, and classifications, "issue treeing" is a wonderful tool for brainstorming, analyzing, organizing, and representing data that can be used to guide student writing. A great tool for creating issue trees is Inspiration (www.inspiration.com).

Lovelycharts (www.lovelycharts.com/gallery). This is a great source to create flowcharts or diagrams. It is a web 2.0 tool and is free. To learn how it works, watch this video: www.lovelycharts.com/screencast.php.

Imagechef (www.imagechef.com). This is a great tool similar to wordcloud, but this one allows you to put in your own words in different shapes. We have used it for creating poetry, specifically shape poems. Here is an example from Maura Brantley:

Prezi. And Prezi is always a good tool. Here's one a group of my students put together for *Lord of the Flies*: prezi.com/0zplpewhyt_a/group-prezi.

Throughout Assignment Sequences and for Culminating Projects

In Rachel's AP English class, she continually uses technology and visual tools. During the year I worked with her, she frontloaded each unit with a PowerPoint presentation including visuals. To frontload the unit on "What work can 'funny' do?" Rachel showed a PowerPoint of cartoons and had students name different kinds of humor, why each example was funny (or not), and what "work" each particular cartoon and kind of humor might do. Additionally, Rachel ran a class wiki, and for this unit she asked students to post something they thought was funny: a cartoon, YouTube video, and so on. Students were asked to view each others' postings and rank the funniest ones, which led to a class discussion and anchor chart classifying kinds of humor and the effects of each. Like all frontloading, this kind of work activates students' prior knowledge and builds on it and, therefore, builds motivation and enthusiasm and prepares students for success with the unit.

Anchor Standards for Reading, 1–9

Anchor Standard for Writing, 4

Rachel is also expert at using visuals and technology in her assignment sequences. Early in her unit on "Whose story gets told?" she helped her students to explore both archetypes and perspective by displaying a painting by Paolo Uccello entitled *St. George and the Dragon*, using this as both a way into a Direct Reading Thinking Activity (DRTA) of a poem "Not My Best Side," and returning to the painting as a touchstone throughout. She found the painting in an online gallery and displayed it using a projector. Note how well Rachel meets CCSS standards for understanding rhetorical stance and how author craft leads to meaning.

DRTA
"Not My Best Side" Archetypes

My Teaching Goals
- Frontload unit on archetypes and perspective.
- Discuss expectations for archetypal hero, villain, and "damsel in distress."
- Engage in small-group and full-class visual analysis,
- Provide introduction to poetry analysis.
- Discuss ways in which authors "manipulate" archetypal characters and their perspectives for particular purposes.

My Frontloading Activities
- Put up image of *Saint George and the Dragon* by Paolo Uccello.
- Hand out a card to each student with either "Maiden," "Dragon," or "Knight" written on it.
- Have each student complete the following tasks for his or her character:
  1. Describe what this character is like.
  2. Describe what he or she did before this moment.
  3. Describe what he or she will do after this moment.
  4. Write a first-person narration of what he or she is thinking at this moment.
  5. Write a first-person narration of what he or she would say to one other character in the painting at this moment.
- Form small groups—one dragon, one maiden, one knight.
  1. Have each group member share his or her narration.
  2. Discuss: "Where do our expectations for these characters come from?"

- With the whole class:
  1. Ask volunteers to share their narration.
  2. Engage in a class discussion of archetypal expectations.

My Previewing and Purpose Setting
- Explain that we will read a poem called "Not My Best Side," which is a direct response to this painting.
- We will consider our expectations for the characters and how they do or do not meet those expectations.
- We will compare and contrast our first-person narrative responses to those presented in the poem.
- We will consider structure, language, and purpose of this poem.

During Reading Responses
(students will receive copies of the poem to annotate one stanza at a time)
Think Aloud
  1. Title
  2. Stanza 1—teacher model
  3. Stanza 2—teacher and students
  4. Stanza 3—in pairs
  5. Full class discussion of stanza 3

After Reading
Questions for Discussion:
  1. In what ways does each speaker reinforce or affirm the assumptions you made about him/her/it?
  2. In what ways does your speaker reject or go against the assumptions you made about him/her/it?
  3. Why is the knight interested most in maintaining the paradigm represented in the painting?

This use of visuals in assignment sequences helps students to develop and use new conceptual and procedural understandings, and is in line with research in cognitive science promoting the use of visuals and concrete hands-on experiences as a way towards abstract thought (for a full discussion, see Wilhelm, et al., 2001).

After this sequence, some students used some of the tools listed below to digitally change the painting or to create new artworks using images from the painting to express their own ideas about the archetypes, gender, male-female relations, and so on.

Artpad (artpad.art.com/artpad/painter/?ic3ebd1jq1lc) allows you to draw your own picture, save it, add to it, and create a video. It can be very fun!

Aviary (www.aviary.com) and Be Funky (www.befunky.com) allow you to upload a photo or jpg image, edit it, save it, and post it!

Draw Island (drawisland.com) is a fun tool because not only can you draw, but you can make it animated, too!

Fontself (www.fontself.com) allows you to type in text, then adjust the font and colors, then save it as a jpg.

We used a lot of these programs with our students, usually introducing a few at a time and showing them how they work, then allowing them some play time. They usually become so enthralled with the technology that they start using them on their own, not only in my class, but in others as well. Oh, and this is barely brushing the surface—there's SO much more out there.

This was something Rachel's students did a lot of: they created parodies, satires, video ads, and videotaped drama scenes/action strategies (see Wilhelm, 2003/2012) in ways that critiqued and transformed the cultural messages expressed through various texts and artwork. This kind of work promotes a deep critical literacy, and helps to meet many aspects of the CCSS.

Rachel is the leader of the Boise State Writing Project CCSS implementation team, and has done prodigious work showing inquiry models of teaching. As a teacher who embraces inquiry, she is always working towards learning performances that provided "proof of purchase" that make student learning visible and justified in actual accomplishment. These culminating projects often used a combination of visuals and technology.

For example, as a culminating project for "Whose story gets told?" many students created video documentaries. My personal favorite was a group of boys who shadowed new immigrants to America from the Sudan and Darfur, interviewing them about their experiences in their homeland and in America about being silenced and how they learned to use their voices. It was a moving video that met the highest standards for video documentary making, and for thinking and using literacy like historians.

In another culminating project on perspective and point of view, Rachel had groups create collaborative multi-modal essays via wikispaces to blend words and images from differing perspectives (including videos and often student-created animated movies through www.xtranormal.com). Her students are always combing the web for more tools and they found a graffiti creator (www.graffiticreator.net) and also a cartoon strip creator (www.pixton.com) that they used to create contributions to these multimodal essays.

In any of these activities, several standards from the CCSS are met. In this instance, these are the ones that were most obviously addressed:

RL.11-12.6. Analyze a case in which grasping a point of view requires distinguishing what is directly stated in a text from what is really meant (e.g., satire, sarcasm, irony, or understatement).

W.11-12.6. Use technology, including the Internet, to produce, publish, and update individual or shared writing products in response to ongoing feedback, including new arguments or information.

SL.11-12.5. Make strategic use of digital media (e.g., textual, graphical, audio, visual, and interactive elements) in presentations to enhance understanding of findings, reasoning, and evidence and to add interest.

SL.11-12.2. Integrate multiple sources of information presented in diverse formats and media (e.g., visually, quantitatively, orally) in order to make informed decisions and solve problems, evaluating the credibility and accuracy of each source and noting any discrepancies among the data.

The examples I present of teachers and students using technology to make meaning are especially exciting because the format and process of each project matches the inquiry, so it shows how the use of technology should be deliberate and purposeful, not just technology for the sake of technology. The class is studying perspective and modes of storytelling and they are creating a piece that tells a story through different modes, addressing the essential question and blending the voices of multiple writers through a collaborative composition.

Video productions were also used as creative projects. As a culminating project for the whole year, my daughter Jasmine and her partner Laura created a very amusing video in which they traveled through "Literature Land," interviewing authors and characters from the various books they had read throughout the course about their responses to different essential questions.

These kinds of projects both develop and consolidate the independent use of various procedural and conceptual understandings. Rachel also challenged students to tell the story of their learning and justify it by exploring *how* they know what they know and why they produced what they produced. This kind of process analysis was sometimes done on video, but more often through writing.

Erika Boas also uses a wide variety of visuals in her teaching, as frontloading, in assignment sequences, and as culminating projects. Erika often has students create flow charts that explore various kinds of relationships among characters, forces, or ideas. These kinds of flow charts are another way for students to compose "process analyses" justifying their thinking.

Here's some for you to play around with:

ToonDoo. Create a comic strip or whole comic book. Lots of backgrounds, characters and styles to choose from.

Create a Graph. Generate five different kinds of graphs from your own data.

MindMeister. A collaborative online mind-mapping tool.

Gliffy. Draw, share, and edit flow charts, diagrams, and technical drawings.

Scriblink. An online collaborative whiteboard.

The example below is a student creation for the novel *Parvana* and was created using Word 2010 and the Smart Art facilities. The software Publisher is useful for this kind of work too.

Erika also has her seventh graders do a wide variety of publishing as part of culminating projects: PSAs, brochures, posters, and the like. This clearly meets some of the important speaking and listening standards in the CCSS regarding publication and presentation.

Erika is also exceptional at documenting student work through digital photography, and by making it archival and available to students. She encourages students to keep a visual record of all their work in their portfolios. The students love using cameras to take images of their posters and projects. When the course is done, students have a transportable record of visual signs of growth and accomplishment that can be carried with them.

This is a habit I wish more teachers would adapt: constantly documenting student work and progress. Beyond the usefulness to Erika as a teacher and teacher-researcher into student learning, she is also constantly valuing her students' work and naming them as readers, composers, and as imaginative and creative people with great potential. It's inspiring to see.

When I observed students engage in such activities, I'm continually struck by the substantive work these students are undertaking, the deep conceptual and procedural learning they display, but perhaps most of all, by the palpable joy with which they do their work. Learning should be a profound kind of "hard fun" and using visuals with tech tools to pursue powerful understandings is a way to support and achieve it.

MAKING THE SCENE!
Seeing and Summarizing Characters, Events, and Situations

One afternoon as I walked out of school, I saw three girls at the corner who were carrying home portraits they had painted of literary characters they had read about this year. They were each holding the portrait in front of their face, and they were interacting as if they were the characters, talking and enlivening their perspectives as they summarized various events and commented about various topics, complete with accents. I stood there for a couple of minutes, laughing silently. They, of course, could not see me, as they kept the portraits in front of their faces. Throughout my career, I have often seen students engage in such activities, sometimes spontaneously, often with a kind of verve and joy.

When I first began this chapter on summarizing, a student named Bambino came to mind. He was part of the boys and literacy study I did with Michael Smith, and an aficionado of the World Wrestling Federation and Extreme Championship Wrestling. Bambino kept an incredibly detailed journal about these shows. During lunch, he would often entertain his classmates by performing a simulated sportscast of the previous night's matches. His classmates depended on his summaries to keep up with the shows. In addition to watching matches on television, Bambino read trade magazines about wrestling, as did Mick, another boy in the study who pretended he was the wrestling character Captain Jack. Ricardo, yet another wrestling fan, often play-acted roles from wrestling shows. He took bets on "Smackdown" (a round of staged championship wrestling bouts), based on the plot conventions that helped him predict what kinds of things would happen. Once, when Ricardo was asked if the wrestling was real, he responded, "No way, man, these are soap operas for guys!" One might say that these young men were doing everything an English teacher would want: they were totally engaged with stories, they could place-hold facts and tell them to others, and they cared about characters and entered into their experience even to the extent of pretending to be a particular character. One of them even wrote to keep

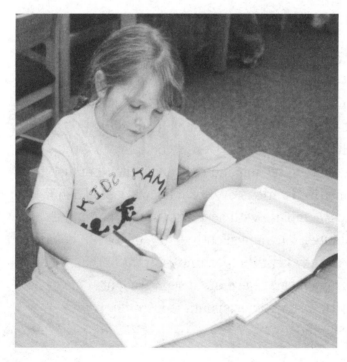

Ask yourself: Do you know your students well enough, as learners and as people, to most effectively teach them?

track of what he had seen. They should have been fantastic English students, but none of them were. Why? They simply weren't willing to put the effort into school that they put into their out-of-school activities. But they might be willing to put forth that effort if only, as we heard again and again, their teachers would "teach me for who I am."

Other students of mine have made similar comments:

> "[School] is not about us. We aren't even in the equation."

> "The teachers don't care about us or our stuff. Why should we care about them or their stuff?"

> "I want to do something that shows who I am. The teachers never let me do that. I am always doing their work instead of my work. So nobody [in the class] can get to know me, I can't show who I am or who I want to be. School is just a waste of time to me and I don't think the teachers are ever going to change."

Comments such as these are unnerving. They prompt me to consider: Do I know my students well enough to teach them? Do I privilege and use what they bring to the table? Do they know I care about them?

**Anchor Standards
for Reading, 1–3**

The young men of our study wanted to be recognized and to make a human connection to their teachers. They wanted to connect personally with the content of the curriculum and to do work that identified themselves as vital, evolving people. These students reminded me that in order to teach well, I must harness the social power of the classroom. This chapter explores how I have tried to do this in using a cluster of visualization techniques around the skills of summarizing and inferring. These strategies allow students to reveal who they are and who they want to be as they interact with characters, settings, and situations in personally meaningful ways.

These strategies help students to:

- notice, identify, and envision key details about characters, situations, and events.

- combine details to create a complete story world or mental model.

- use visualized details to create summaries.

- connect and synthesize details to make various kinds of inferences.

- use visual details as tools to think with, construct, and interpret implied textual meanings.

The Skill at Hand: Inferencing

First, let me define inferencing, the skill all techniques in this chapter ultimately lead to. Inferencing is an essential element of all sophisticated reading tasks, particularly tasks where we read to learn or understand something new. It involves the ability to see connections, relationships, and patterns between various details and parts of a single text. But readers also need to make inferences between texts and beyond texts. These relationships might be between the world and the text, between one's personal experience and the text, or between similar texts or texts about the same topic. Inferencing is essential to creating knowledge in math, science, or any other discipline. It is an essential element of achieving many of the Common Core State Standards in English-Language Arts and in literacy in the disciplines.

George Hillocks (1980) cites several kinds of relationships between text details that the accomplished reader must discern and understand in order to make inferences. Authors often use a "directly stated relationship" between two or more ideas. This is literally presented information and does not require making an inference. Nonetheless, readers must identify and remember the connection, which is typically causal. More sophisticated and challenging are what Hillocks calls "simple implied relationships." In these, the separate details are close to each other in the text and provide different pieces of information about a similar idea or theme. It is up to the reader to discover the nature of the relationship between the pieces of information.

"Complex implied relationships" occur when a reader must connect a large number and variety of different details spread across different parts of the text (or across different texts in an in-depth inquiry, such as understanding history, legal precedents, or different points of view). To make such inferences, students must be able to "identify the necessary details, discern whatever patterns exist among them, and then draw the appropriate inference from the nature of the pattern" (Hillocks, 1980, p. 308). This is something that fewer than six percent of American high school seniors can do, and it is essential to creating knowledge and new understandings while reading.

"Authorial generalizations" (a central-focus statement for a text) must be inferred unless an author directly states his or her main point (which rarely happens, particularly in literary texts). This requires students to infer and articulate the main point a text implies about a particular topic. Students must consider "the proposition(s) that the story might be said to represent" (Hillocks, 1980, p. 308).

Finally, there are "structural generalizations," an explanation of how a text is constructed to make a particular point and how the various parts of a text work together to make that point. "[This] requires the reader to explain how parts of the work operate together to achieve certain effects" (Hillocks, 1980, p. 308). Authors never explain how their texts are structured to emphasize and highlight these effects and ideas, so these insights must always be inferred. All of these achievements are essential elements of the CCSS.

Anchor Standards for Reading, 1–6, 8

The ability to see connections and infer their meaning is a complex and incredibly important set of skills. But inferencing depends on the ability to identify key details and to bring these forward throughout a reading so they can be connected to new key details to see patterns of meaning. In this way, summarizing is a skill upon which all other higher levels of interpretation and thinking depend. To introduce and hone all of these skills with your students, try beginning with an entry point that Bambino and his buddies would approve of: delving into character. It's a starting point that builds nicely on the frontloading techniques explored earlier, as these techniques start with the known—an exploration of the student's character—and then connect to the new—to unfamiliar characters, ideas, and authors of texts. Understanding the known and the literal is a prerequisite to understanding the new and the implied.

Understanding Character

Understanding character is essential to comprehending a fictional text. To get any satisfaction from a story or novel, a reader must understand what motivates characters, how they change over time, how they relate to each other, and how their interactions and motivations drive the plot. And readers must also understand where characters stand at a story's end.

Character is also important in historical narrative and informational texts. After all, human history is the story of people's experiences through different times, contexts, and events, and these personal experiences resonate with young readers.

In my studies for *You Gotta BE the Book* (1997/2008), *Teaching for Love and Wisdom* (2011), and *Imagining to Learn* (1998), I found that good readers often insert context and character into texts where this element is missing or only implied. For example, when reading a word problem that involves a recipe, a reader might imagine himself actually preparing that recipe. When reading an essay in favor of wearing school uniforms, a reader tends to create a sense of the author and actively contend with her. In my latest research from *Teaching for Love and Wisdom*, I explore how students also posit implied authors and converse with them.

Hello, Author

When students connect with the author and consider the intelligence behind the text, they begin to read in a more engaged and "dialogic" fashion. Encourage them to ask questions during and after reading, such as:

- Who wrote this?

- Why did she write it?

- For whom did she write it?

- What is the point of the writing? What kind of thinking or social action is it intended to promote?

Exploring questions such as these is central to critical reading.

The benefits of this peopling and personalizing of texts are great. When character—or a pronounced authorial perspective—is made part of informational-text reading, the reader's meaning-making is energized by this human dimension. Indeed, I've found that students strive to imagine a human need or function that can be played out with the information they are reading (Smith & Wilhelm, 2002; Wilhelm, 1997/2008; Wilhelm & Edmiston, 1998).

Activities That Help Students to Infer Character

This first group of activities helps students to infer character. The strategies also help students to make other kinds of inferences related to characters—about settings, a character's relationships to others, historical periods, situations—and to pay attention to visual details that can be resources during their reading. The beauty of these strategies is that everybody can see, hear, and assist each other's reading and thinking processes, as students work on these projects together and then present them.

Blueprint for Introducing All the Techniques

Below is a series of steps to keep in mind as you use the strategies for summarizing and inferring with your students.

1 Model your use of a visualization strategy with a text excerpt.

2 Have students read the next text passage aloud, silently, in pairs, or in small groups. Encourage them to keep in mind and use what you have modeled.

3 Brainstorm—either as a whole class or in small groups—to list salient images, details, or scenes on the board or chart paper.

4 Discuss how everyone pictures the details, scenes, and characters and why each person envisions the scene as he does.

5 Create a visual artifact (individually or in groups) to capture some aspect of textual meaning.

6 Share and discuss visual artifacts, noticing how they are alike and different; articulating what they express about the text's meaning; and looking to see if there are patterns that show up across the artifacts.

In step 6, I often have students post their work and then walk around to view it. Sometimes I ask them to write questions or comments on a clipboard posted next to each artifact. We then use these notes to fuel a class discussion. As a variation, I invite half the class to walk around while the other half sits with their work and discusses it with their "wandering" classmates, then have them switch roles. After this activity, students can read the rest of the text, alone or in pairs, and try to use the modeled technique.

Personality Profile

At the beginning of the school year, have students write personality profiles of themselves. You might also pair students to write profiles of each other, which has the benefit of allowing students to get to know each other while they learn to conduct an interview, check facts, and write a compelling profile.

Students can create PowerPoint slides about themselves that include scanned or digital photos of themselves involved in favorite activities or in a favorite context. My students sometimes include audio files of favorite songs and video clips of themselves or of friends talking about them. But whether done as a writing assignment or a high-tech presentation, this activity works nicely as an ice-breaker for students—and it's a great way to review the aspects of character that must be understood by a reader, including:

- Physical appearance
- Typical dress
- Favorite activities
- Favorite books, movies, music
- Modes of speech and language used
- Ways of interacting with others
- Personal quotes, ways of talking
- Beliefs and opinions
- Emotions and reactions
- Soapbox topics (strong beliefs)
- Favorite places and typical surroundings
- Friends and other social relationships/groups belonged to
- Responses of significant others
- Quotes from others about them

"Give Me the Story"

"Maybe I would read a person's story about slavery and how they get through. Yeah, that sounds pretty good, but I don't want to read about the whole timeline of slavery..." Geo says it all. Students are drawn to the stories of individuals, not disembodied facts. And research bears this out. Character is highly important to student reading interest and engagement (Wilhelm, 1997/2008; Smith & Wilhelm, 2002).

Students build knowledge about character and character-ization as they work together to write per-sonality profiles (see also Smith & Wilhelm, 2009, 2010).

Extending the Profile

Use a website or wiki to extend, share, and build on the personality profile throughout the year. For example, students can add details regarding a character, author, or idea—for a character, a student describes how the character's appearance is similar to or different from his own, how the character's beliefs differ with or are similar to his own, or how the character experiences relationships in ways similar to the student. To extend an author detail, a student articulates how an author's attitudes seem similar to or different from her own, which requires understanding authorial generalizations. And to extend an idea, a student expresses how a text sparked or developed an idea, or how his understanding of an issue was transformed through the reading.

What Students Had to Say: Joe, a seventh grader, after plugging characters from *Roll of Thunder, Hear My Cry* (Taylor, 1976) into his personality-profile, wrote:

> I learned that I am a lot like Cassie because I get offended when I
> am treated unfairly. But I learned I am better off than her because
> my family is not going to get killed if I stand up for myself, which
> was something that could happen to her back then. And I learned
> that there are different ways of dealing with problems. Like Papa
> always made a plan to solve problems through the back door,
> by being smart and tricky. Mr. Morrison used physical strength,

but he was quiet about it. Uncle Hammer used anger and putting it in people's faces. Putting them [these characters] in my profile made me realize I am most like Uncle Hammer, which surprised me, but I think it is smarter to be more like Papa, so I am going to think about how to be more like that.

The possibilities for building on personality profiles and the benefits of doing so are many. At the end of the year, the students will have a sophisticated wiki or website that shows how they have connected to the various characters, authors, and ideas encountered throughout the year. They will have also deeply explored what makes us human and marks our identity as well as various ways of being in the world. To me, this is one of the major purposes of reading and of a democratic education.

Body Bios

I first learned about body bios at an NCTE conference, and it has become a favorite of my students ever since. In this activity, which is very much a grown-up version of the classic kindergarten activity, students trace their bodies on long sheets of butcher paper. They then color in the forms using a variety of symbols and labels. There are many methods of filling in the forms, one of which is creating an anatomically-based biography. In this type of body bio, the brain area is used as a place to put images about the subject's interests, personal knowledge, and expertise. The heart area is where emotional attachments, passions, strong opinions, and feelings are symbolically portrayed. At the eyes, favorite books and movies might be portrayed along with a representation of how the individual typically sees the world. At the stomach, favorite foods are shown, and at the mouth, the subject's typical style of language. Arms and legs are used to show favorite activities, and so on. The area of the paper surrounding the figure could be used to visually describe favorite places or typical surroundings. As with the hypermedia project, I like to have students create a biography of themselves and then one of a character or author, which is a more challenging endeavor. They can then use the biographies to forge connections with characters, comparing similarities and differences in backgrounds, concerns, situations, strengths, and weaknesses.

Katie Hutchison's portrait of Cassie Logan, which she embedded into a profile about her family and how they compare to the Logan family.

DVD

Before, During, or After Reading: Body Biography

What Students Had to Say: After sixth grader Sarah created a body biography for herself, and then a parallel one for Annemarie of *Number the Stars* (Lowry, 1992), she wrote:

> [Doing] this kind of slaps you in the face and wakes you up! I never thought much about what a potty mouth I am, and how much junk food I eat. Wow! And this made me think even more when I compared myself to Annemarie, who had no junk food to eat, and who had to be loyal and true to her friends and family or they could all die. Maybe her responsibilities made her that way, that good and that serious. Maybe I don't have enough responsibility? (Don't tell my mom!) It made me think that I am a big softie and I better get it together. If I had to live through what Annemarie did, I don't know if I could do it.

Dressed-Up Body Bios

Other students I've taught have clothed the figure created in the body bio activity and then surrounded it with symbols and biographical details. Everything they chose resonated with deep meaning about their character. Details might include props, accessories, jewelry, characteristic colors, and quotations from and about the character. Other writing on and around the figure can be used to reveal the character's virtues and vices, concerns, obstacles faced, major ideas, significant others, typical actions and activities, and defining moments.

What Students Had to Say: Tanya, a seventh grader, offered a powerful insight about this activity when she told me the following:

> You know how you are always talking about making our reading and thinking visible so we can test it out? Well, I think the dressed-up body bio is great because it makes us as people visible to each other.... I like that. It's like I'm finally learning about other people, and with them and from them instead of sitting all alone at a desk.

Name Tags

Teacher Sharon Stein at the Rutgers Writing Project introduced this simple technique to me. On the first day of school, Sharon has students create their own large name tags that represent themselves—their strengths, interests, feelings, and so on—through art. She provides them with a variety of materials to use for decorating their name tags, such as glitter, markers, wrapping paper, and buttons. The twist is that their names cannot appear on the name tag. Students create their name tags without looking at each other's work. When everyone is finished, each student pulls one tag out of a box where they have been placed. In turn, each student shows the class the tag they drew from the box. The class studies the tag, lists the details they see, and draws inferences about the person who created it and what they were trying to communicate. The point is not to guess the name or person who created the name tag, but simply to make inferences about the creator. The student presenting the name tag sums up the inferences made. When the discussion of a particular tag is complete, the student asks who made the name tag and delivers it back to her.

You might also give students the names of different characters or authors the class has read about and ask them to make a name tag for the character or author of their choice. Then have students present the name tags, making inferences to guess who from the unit the name tags symbolized.

Jasmine's name tag for Count Olaf from Lemony Snicket's *A Series of Unfortunate Events*. The mask shows that he is a master of disguise, the dollar bill shows his greed, the black car shows his mobility and penchant for showing up "at the wrong place at the right time." The "eye" is his tattoo.

Jasmine's personal name tag, showing her interests in playing basketball, running, softball, reading, playing the clarinet, love of pizza and animals. She has added her name after the tag was presented to the class.

Self-Portraits/Portfolio Folders

Kip Plaisted, a teacher at our national demonstration site for adolescent literacy in Washington County, Maine, has his students create a self-portrait which they use to adorn their portfolio folder. He then has them decorate their folders in the same manner as the name tags in the above activity. Kip's students also fill out an interest survey that he uses throughout the year to monitor how well he is meeting student interest, and to guide him in suggesting free-reading choices and so on. The completed survey is laminated and placed inside the folder. The outside of the folder is therefore a visual expression of each student's personality, and the inside of the folder is a written expression of that students needs and interests. The folder itself will hold the work that the student completes throughout the year, marking his or her growth and identity.

Picture Talk

One of my favorite techniques for helping students infer character is something I call a picture talk. I simply find photographs of interesting-looking characters. Then I show students a photograph and ask them to make inferences about the character of the person in the photograph based solely on the visual details. One of my best sources for doing this is a photo book of candid portraits taken during the sixties—kids love the photos of hippies, policemen, and students with their bell bottoms.

Imagine these two characters meeting. Where might they meet? What would they say to each other?

To get them started making inferences about such characters, I might prompt them to:

- Freewrite: identify anything you see and what you think it might help you know about this person.

- Describe the person.

- Imagine what he or she is looking at.

- Imagine what he or she is thinking. Put it in the person's own words as a stream of consciousness.

- Imagine what this person's job is.

- Decide where this person lives. What is his or her favorite hangout?

- Describe what this person will eat for dinner.

- Imagine what this person's nickname is.

- Decide what this person's favorite movie, book, or song might be.

- Imagine what this person's soapbox topic (something he or she cares intensely about) might be.

- Write a brief monologue about this topic from the person's perspective, using his or her language.

In each case, I ask students to justify their inference. What in the picture, and in their own personal experience, might lead them to their conclusions? We talk about the need to justify inferences, the necessity of keeping initial inferences tentative and open to revision, and how inferences need to be confirmed by various sources of information. We also discuss what we need to observe and know about these characters to have confidence in our inferences. Then the fun begins: I put two photos together and ask students to make inferences about the relationship between them. The more incongruous or provocative the pairing, the better—put a hippie with a dress-suited, conservative-looking person, for example. I prompt students to consider:

- Where might these two meet?

- In what situations might they meet?

- What are they thinking when they see each other?

- Who begins the conversation?

- What does he or she say?

- How does the other person respond?

I then ask students to write down their imagined dialogue between the two characters, and they always have a blast with this. They must justify what they have written by naming the visual cues that inspired them. I then explain how we must visualize characters and make these same kinds of inferences based on the textual cues we get during reading. As a variation, I might present photographs of people who look similar to characters in a novel we are reading and link that activity to the book.

Picture Talk Variation: Historic Photographs

During a unit on the Great Depression, my students explored this inquiry question: "What happens when the structures in one's life break down?" Students tried to understand what it must have been like to have no money, to lose a family house and farm, and to have siblings go far away to find work. We studied and responded to WPA photos of people and asked: Who are these people? What might their names and ages be? Are they related? What are they doing? How are they feeling? What does the head of the household do? What are their plans? What do we foresee for their futures?

We also studied photos of settings without characters, asking: What is this place? Who might live here? Why does the place look as it does? What events have happened here? What might happen? What conflict might happen here?

In this Great Depression unit, we used two books by Elizabeth Partridge. The first is a biography of Dorothea Lange for young people called *Restless Spirit*, which includes photographs of Lange and reproductions of famous photos. The other is Partridge's book about Woody Guthrie called *This Land Belongs to You and Me*, which includes his songs, photos, and drawings. Finally we used the book *Something Permanent* by Cynthia Rylant, which matches her original poetry to classic WPA photos.

Picture Talk Variation: Postcards

Postcards, art postcards, or prints of paintings can also be used with the picture talk technique. Sharon Stein uses art postcards and asks students to do the following:

- Tell a story about a character in the painting.

- Respond as the person in the painting: Why did you pose this way? What were you communicating about yourself and your situation? How happy are you with the painting? Tell us your life story as the person in the painting.

- Create a dialogue with a character from another painting.

Great Books That Use Visuals

Prairie Visions: The Life and Times of Solomon Butcher by Pam Conrad features archival photographs taken by pioneer Butcher to punctuate narrative vignettes from pioneers.

Kids at Work: Lewis Hine and the Crusade Against Child Labor by Russell Freedman uses archival photographs by Hine, which he took to document the horrors of child labor. This book is a good example of how visual information can be a form of social action.

Romare Bearden: Collage of Memories by Jan Greenberg and Romare Bearden is a dynamite biography of African-American artist Bearden. It features various Bearden compositions with companion text.

Steamboat! The Story of Captain Blanche Leathers by Judith Gilliland is a fascinating picture book biography of the first female river steamboat captain.

Hottest, Coldest, Highest, Deepest by Steve Jenkins depicts the most extreme places on our planet using collage illustrations.

The Top of the World: Climbing Mount Everest by Steve Jenkins includes stunning photographs of climbers and the Himalayas.

Tuesday by David Wiesner uses triptychs of illustrations to show action at different points. It's great for teaching perspective and sequences.

Sundiata by David Wisniewski offers a brilliant use of composition to get across setting and action.

Sumo Mouse by David Wisniewski, presented in a comic book format, demonstrates various ways of telling narrative and using motifs. It's great for teaching inferencing based on visual patterns.

More Activities for Exploring Character

Yearbook Pages

DVD

Before and During Reading: Concrete Objects/ Precious Objects (a version of Yearbook Pages)

To help students delve into how characters express and portray identity, assign them the task of creating the yearbook pages for various characters. As a senior yearbook page might, these pages can include favorite activities, classes taken, leadership roles, friends, and seminal events. I sometimes have my students assume the role of the character whose yearbook page they designed and sign each other's pages in that role. Bind all of the pages together into a Book Yearbook.

A character yearbook

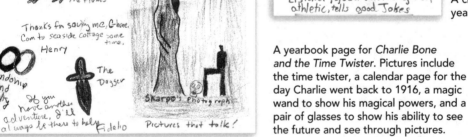

A yearbook page for *Charlie Bone and the Time Twister*. Pictures include the time twister, a calendar page for the day Charlie went back to 1916, a magic wand to show his magical powers, and a pair of glasses to show his ability to see the future and see through pictures.

Illustrated Character Journals

In or out of role, students can create character diaries or journals and illustrate these with drawings, magazine cutouts, clip art, and so on. These can be respectful, but sometimes students cannot resist making them satiric, making their descriptions comic or humorously critical.

Character Interests/Emotional Displays

In an idea several of my student-teachers have adapted from Phyllis Whitin's excellent book *Sketching Stories, Stretching Minds* (1996), kids can be asked to create a pie graph of their own average day, interests, and emotional make-up and then to create one for a character, so they can compare and discuss what these findings show about personality and values. Students also enjoy adapting this idea to create self and character stress-o-meters (showing how different situations cause different levels of stress, reactions, and so on), value line graphs (the various degree to which values are embraced or displayed by a character or author) and Chinese nest boxes that display the difference between outward appearance and values and inner ones. These techniques can also be used to explore and display the emphases, focus on various characters, values, emotional content, ideas, and themes expressed by a book. Again, these decisions should be justified based on textual evidence.

Melinda's pie graph shows how she spends her time on a typical day.

Character Symbol Maps

Maps of character values before and then after a story can be powerful ways to show character change. I recently asked my students to create such maps for the character Eustace after a reading of C.S. Lewis's *Voyage of the Dawn Treader*. I prompted them to justify the values they identified with evidence from the text. At the end they explained what events were most important in Eustace's transformation.

After Reading: Precious Object Leading to a Picture Map (a variation of Character Symbol Maps)

This symbol map shows that Tintin has a sense of adventure (ship), is brave (the sword), loves to travel (thumbs up), has a quick, explosive personality (TNT), many hidden talents (locked trunk), a loyal dog (Snowy, his dog), knowledge (book), likes clean living (overturned liquor bottle), has a great-hearted kindness and love of justice (heart), the ability to be amazed, ask questions, and make plans of action (thought bubble).

Character Wardrobe/Fashion Show

Teacher Kathy Salkaln has her students create character wardrobes from magazine cutouts and asks them to explain how this wardrobe shows the character's values, social class, historical period, or inner traits. This could, of course, also lead to dress-up book reports or dress-up tea parties for characters from the same or different texts.

Applying Character Inferencing to Student Writing

Subtexting Strategy

This is a wonderful technique that I learned from Jean Anne Clyde (Clyde, Barber, Hogue, & Wasz, 2006) that helps students to revise their compositions. This technique builds on student work inferring character. There are three steps in using subtexting to revise:

1. Visualize an imagined reader—the person who represents the audience for the piece. If writing to a specific person (e.g., the school's principal, a character from the book you are reading), compose a brief summary of what you know about her and then visualize her and imagine her stance towards reading your composition.

2. Reread the piece in role *as* that reader, recording her "subtext"—what she is thinking to herself as she reads.

3. Use the imagined reader's comments and questions to guide the revision of the text. Then apply the Subtext Strategy as you review your next draft. Stop when your imaginary reader is fully satisfied.

Picturing content

Flannery O'Connor reportedly told her students to think about three things when they wrote and revised: Voice (style and personality of the voice we hear in our head when we read and when we write), Pictures (ideas/content), and Flow (organization). Voice involves word choice, sentence patterns and personality. Pictures pertain to topic development, evidence, content, substance, proof. Flow is organization, sense of task and audience

I've had good luck with asking students to create picture maps of their own writing, and that of peers during the revision process. It helps students to answer the question: Are there specific pictures when you write? In other words, is there intriguing content for your audience to visualize?

Understanding: Settings, Events, and Ideas

Settings, situations, events, and ideas are used by authors to advance their message. Authors of all texts make choices about what details to include, highlight, or describe in a text. They make these choices strategically for the purpose of communicating and promoting particular ideas to their readers. This next set of techniques delves into understanding situations and settings, and the ideas the author is portraying through them. We will look at the first, tableaux, in several variations.

Anchor Standards for Reading, 1–5

Tableaux

Tableau—a French term for a scene that captures the sweep of a significant moment— has been a favorite technique of mine for a long time. A tableau is versatile, and kids quickly grasp its various uses. I often use tableaux as a drama technique in which groups create "body pictures" or statues with physical stances and gestures that portray story events, relationships, or thematic meanings (see Wilhelm 2003/2012). I also use this as a visual art technique, which I describe here.

After Reading: Introduction to Tableaux

Though I sometimes have students create a single tableau, I more often have them work together to create a series of tableaux that requires them to choose and represent key details, see relationships and patterns across details and scenes, and summarize the whole coherence of ideas or events presented through a particular text segment.

To make tableaux more purposeful, I usually have the groups who are creating them read different texts than the rest of the class, or I make them experts by having them focus their tableaux on a particular part, idea, or motif from a shared class reading. The group must consider what it is the rest of the class must know from this text and how to best depict it so their audience will learn and remember useful information.

For example, during a Civil War unit, groups read different stories from various perspectives. A group reading the story "The Soldier Who Wouldn't Tell" created five scenes that summarized the tale and presented them to the rest of the class. I asked them to conclude their presentation with a statement of what the meaning of the story was and how this made a comment on the Civil War.

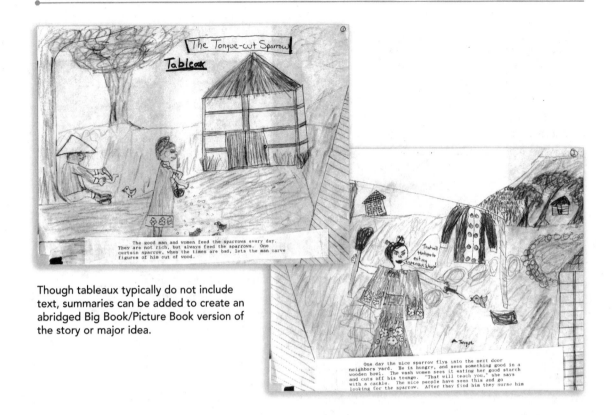

Though tableaux typically do not include text, summaries can be added to create an abridged Big Book/Picture Book version of the story or major idea.

The students struggled a bit to express a statement, so I asked them if there was a theme running across each of the pictures they had created. Here is an excerpt of their conversation, which shows how the tableau work encourages students to start talking about ideas and themes:

"Sam [Davis] never questioned what was the right thing to do, and he stuck with it...I would totally disagree with him [i.e., with Sam's unswerving devotion to the Confederate cause and his sense of loyalty to a Union traitor]," said Josh.

Sharon added, "Maybe that was the problem. I admired Sam a lot, and I showed that in my picture, but the story showed how no one would budge from his beliefs that really came from where they grew up. And that their state was more important to them then being in the U.S. Funny and weird. But that is probably why there was a war."

"Yeah, no one would compromise," Elisha agreed.

This led to a discussion as to whether and when compromise is a good thing, and when it cannot be accepted. Was Sam Davis in a situation where he could not compromise? The students decided that he was.

"If he had [changed his mind about betraying the Confederacy], he couldn't have gone back to his family," Josh opined.

"Wow!" remarked Sharon. "This is really helping me understand why the Civil War happened."

On the next page, you'll find a reproducible guide that takes students step by step through the process of creating a tableau. Feel free to adapt it as you wish.

Summary of "The Soldier Who Wouldn't Tell"

In this true story from the Civil War, retold by George Morrill, Tennessee volunteer Sam Davis is enlisted as a spy to help the Confederacy overcome the Union siege of Vicksburg. Sam obtains sensitive documents from a Union authority who secretly sympathizes with the South. Sam's mother sews the documents into his shoes, and he rides off to deliver the important materials to his generals but is caught by Union pickets. They rip open his shoes and find the documents, and Sam is sentenced to be hanged as a spy. But a Union general (see tableau opposite) is so impressed with his loyalty and integrity that he begs Sam to reveal the traitor who gave him the documents, saying, "He is not worth losing your life for." But Sam refuses, thinking this would be a betrayal of trust and of his cause. The offer is repeated on the gallows; Sam again refuses and is hanged.

A tableau of the penultimate scene of the story.

Tableaux Directions for Narrative Texts

Working in Groups

1. Choose the text or text segment that you wish to depict and visually share with your audience.

2. Consider why the audience will be interested in the text you have read and what they will need to know about it.

3. **Review the important scenes and details your audience will need to know from each scene.** Please consider the journalist's five W's and H (Who, What, Where, When, Why, and How). Remember that the author signals us to notice particular scenes: the first and last ones, those that are surprising, scenes that signal a climax or change in direction, those that offer new and important information, ones that are different in some way, and those that are described in great detail.

Challenge

Use as few details or scenes as possible to communicate the whole story or meaning of a text.

4. Brainstorm how to present these scenes visually in a way that will communicate all the important details of the scene to the audience.

5. **Create visual depictions of the scenes on newsprint sheets.** Make notes on the back about what you need to point out to the audience about each scene. For example, you might include a topic word, write a one-sentence summary of the scene, explain how this scene connects to a prior or following tableau, point out key details and explain how these details are important, cite the theme—or deep meaning—of the scene, or relate this theme to the topic of the excerpt.

6. When you are done with your individual tableau, check to be sure that your audience will completely understand and "see" the event of a meaning of this section of the text.

7. **Rehearse your presentation of the series of tableaux as a group, making sure everyone is involved.** Make sure the tableaux work together to summarize the whole story and sequence of events.

8. Present it!

9. Get feedback on how well you did and what you could do to improve your presentation.

Idea Tableaux

Tableaux lend themselves particularly well to helping students remember and recreate scenes from a narrative. However, tableaux can also depict more abstract textual elements, such as main ideas, motifs, or themes. They can be used to amplify the ideas or text structures of fiction and nonfiction texts or any other kind of non-narrative text. Students can be assigned an excerpt and asked to depict a major point that the reader must carry away from that excerpt. Students can create characters that personify a concept, such as greed or competition or patience, and invent contexts or settings in order to personalize and communicate the meaning of informational texts.

THE CAY REVISITED

OBJECTIVES: To represent your understanding of key details, central focus and personal response to the novel <u>The Cay</u> through writing, illustrating, and selecting appropriate music to accompany the performance of an epilogue.

SCENARIO: Philip hopes someday to return to the cay. Imagine that you are Philip and have returned ten years later. In the form of an epilogue, write a description of your experiences as you revisit the cay. An epilogue is a speech or poem that is presented to the audience at the end of a play by one of the actors. Write the epilogue in a conversation-like style as if you were sharing your feelings with a friend.

STEPS: Divide the epilogue into four parts.

1. The first part should describe briefly how you remember the cay and what happened there.

2. The second part should describe how the cay has changed.

3. The third part should describe your feelings about returning to the cay.

4. The final part should describe how your experiences on the cay changed your life.

IMPLEMENTATION:

- Select a different piece of background music to accompany each part of the epilogue.

- Illustrate each part of the epilogue.

- Present the epilogue, music, and illustrations to the class.

Slide Shows

Students can use PowerPoint or other software to make simple slide shows of tableaux. These can be very sparse and symbolic, or highly detailed and realistic. Just as a traveler wants to show the key places and events of a trip to her friends, students creating these slide shows will depict the central scenes or ideas from a text. Their slide shows will convey the important sights and seminal moments that capture the essence of their reading experience. They might even animate or blend the scenes together to give the audience a dynamic sense of their journey through a text. These slide shows scaffold readers' consideration of key details; as they share them with each other, they discuss why certain details are key, what needs to be included, and what is lost if a particular slide is deleted. In this way, the kids learn a lot from each other about identifying key details and creating summaries.

Teacher Allison Pomerville's elaborated tableaux with music idea.

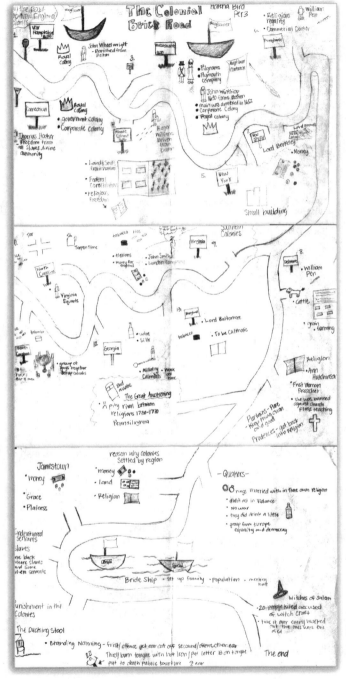

Flow Charts

Having students create flow charts is a very versatile activity that can be used to depict complicated sequences, causal relationships, character development, and the development of various historical trends, debates, or ideas. Flow charts can pictorially show sequence and cause and effect. They can also help students to see the various possibilities—the "what ifs" and choices made at particular times. Flow charts can also explore "roads not taken."

Maps

This next idea comes from Peter Smagorinsky's excellent book *Expressions* (1991). Have students make maps of physical locales as small as a room or as large as the country in which a story or text events take place. Students might also make maps of characters' physical, psychological,

Halena Bird's flow chart displays what she learned about the colonial experience in America. "This is so much better than a test," she commented. "I can see that I understand it, and the drawing helped me to understand it even more. I'm going to remember this!" These last few techniques work great with the narrative, expository and argument texts foregrounded by the CCSS.

or spiritual journeys. In the case of quests, Peter asks students to visually depict the sort of terrain over which the hero journeys (this could of course be metaphorical or symbolic), the major events, the sequence of events and how one led to another, and the direction in which the hero travels. He also uses a "mirror map" strategy by asking students to visually depict their own life quest and compare this to that of the hero.

Roll Movies

Though electronic video technologies and iMovies can do the same thing as old-fashioned roll movies, students often enjoy creating a version or timeline of a story's events on a single sheet. They can then run this sheet as a scroll through a homemade shoebox viewer. Of course, doing it with iMovie or other software is also grand!

Detective Sketches

My long-time team-teaching partner, Paul Friedemann, likes to assign different students to be "police artists" to do detective sketches as they read. The police artist's job is to recreate a past event or series of events, or sketch out what a suspect (historical figure or character) looks like based on the available text details. By compiling the sketches made by various students over the course of a text, or the study of an event (like the battle of Gettysburg and its aftermath), a class winds up with a tableau book that features a story's major characters, scenes, or points. Students greatly enjoy this detective work, and this activity highlights the importance of using background information to make inferences and then to revise ideas based on newly presented information. Paul likes to show students important primary texts and historical documents like Sneden's *Eye of the Storm* (2000) to illustrate how observers of historical events—in this case, a private in the Union army— contribute to our understanding through diaries, sketches, pictures, illustrations, and more.

Some young adult and children's books that fit such a unit are Jim Murphy's *The Boys' War* and *Road to Gettysburg*, Clinton Cox's *Fiery Vision: The Life and Death of John Brown*, and Raymond Bial's *Underground Railroad*, which introduces a different view of John Brown than that offered in Cox's book.

Great Books

Other historical texts that use primary documents, photos, and drawings include:

Anne Frank: Beyond the Diary by Ruud van der Rol and Rian Verhoeven. Ancillary materials and documents about Anne's life.

At Her Majesty's Request by Walter Dean Myers. True story of an African Princess who was Queen Victoria's ward, contrasts different cultural views of leadership.

The Planet Hunters by Dennis Trodin Franklin. Explores the discovery of Pluto.

Where the Action Was by Penny Colman. Women War Correspondents in WWII.

Shipwreck at the Bottom of the World by Jennifer Armstrong. Shackleton's amazing voyage of survival.

Through My Eyes by Ruby Bridges. Multiple perspectives on correspondent Ruby Bridges.

We Were There Too! by Phillip Hoose. Children's role in American history with archival illustrations.

Studying Illustrated Texts

Carefully selected cartoons, picture books, and other illustrated texts can be used to teach many reading strategies, from understanding and visualizing key details to inferring character to understanding irony and symbolism. For example, in Ludwig Bemelman's well-loved Madeline books, settings are depicted with colorful tableaux while actions are shown with line drawings. When I show these books to students, I ask: "What is important for an illustrator to depict? What can be imagined? How much must be depicted? What cues does the viewer or reader need to be able to fill in the blanks? What do we need to know to imagine a setting versus imagining a character? How do different techniques work to convey different story aspects?" Discussions around such questions help students to not only attend and critically appreciate illustrations, but to think about them in a writerly way—as a method of communication.

Janet Stevens' book *Tops and Bottoms* explores the Brer Rabbit story in a calendar format. Students can study the effect of her playful line work, and how the calendar framing structures their experience of the text. Her book *From Pictures to Words: a Book About Making a Book* looks at the choices authors and illustrators make in creating a book.

In *To Fly: The Story of the Wright Brothers*, Wendie Old uses a variety of visual techniques to show the brothers' collaboration, experimentation, moods, and the settings and salient elements of the context in which they worked.

Illustrating Texts

My students enjoy providing illustrations for non-illustrated text. This technique helps them to visualize from print—to notice and flesh out important details and scenes. Sometimes I ask the class to provide illustrations for a chapter or for a whole text. Their job is to decide what is important in the assigned excerpt and what are the most effective ways to visually highlight this important information. I have always had students draw pictures, flow charts, graphs, and other visuals, but now that I have computers and a digital camera, I also encourage them to stage photographs, dress them up with Adobe Photoshop, and create other computer graphics.

Summary Texts With Illustrated Commentary

To help students summarize and bring accrued meanings forward, I often have them create summaries of texts they have read independently to share with each other. I sometimes prompt them to create illustrated sidebar commentaries for the following categories: frightening facts, definitions, culture corner, Did you know?, related statistics, related readings, and implied social action projects.

Picture Book Summaries/Big Books

The task of boiling a longer and more complex text down into a picture book helps students to conceive of how to summarize and visually represent ideas from more complicated texts. I've often arranged for my students to adopt reading buddies from lower grades whom they meet with and tutor on various occasions throughout the year. This context makes creating a picture book very real for them; their job is to summarize something they've learned for their reading buddy in a way that stimulates interest and helps the younger student to comprehend a story or idea. Students have created excellent summaries of not only stories but also sophisticated concepts, like Newton's laws of motion.

Students can also create what I call "big books"—large picture book summaries. These are alternative versions that might be an iteration from an alternate perspective, an elaboration or extension of a story, or a satire, recasting, or otherwise "twisted" version of a text. Students enjoy inserting themselves and their friends into a text as characters or commentators, which adds the human dimension and connection everyone seeks in reading.

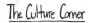

The Culture Corner

The Navajo raised sheep, cultivated their gardens of corn and watermelon, and tended their fruit orchards. Only women owned sheep, a sign of wealth among them, and an indication of their desirability for marriage. Men, on the other hand, hunted deer and warred with other tribes...

This was the Navajo way...

Bright Morning was happy. Spring had finally come, and she had been allowed to take the sheep to their grazing pastures high above the valley that was her home. She was the first of any of the village girls—she had gotten up extra early to make sure she'd be the first to arrive—and so it was her right to give greetings to the next girl who should arrive.

Being the first to give greetings was a matter of pride—something Bright Morning had lost when her mother had taken away her sheep-herding privileges last year. Now Bright Morning knew better than to leave the sheep alone and defenseless, even if a frightening and unexpected Spring snow storm should happen again!

All winter, Bright Morning had dreamt of sheep.

This year was different. This year, not only was Bright Morning allowed to again tend the flocks, she had been given sheep of her very own.

Looking over the flocks, Bright Morning was so happy she wanted to dance—but she remained stoic. Nor did she make known her love for Tall Boy, the arrogant young warrior her father would likely arrange to have her marry when her Islands Wanted to cross...

Frightening Fact:

Spanish slavers often stole young women from the Navajo tribes and sold them in their towns. As it was the men of the tribe who rode horses, the girls then found it very difficult to escape—even if they stole a horse...

Black Dog lay still...

The days passed one to the next as Bright Morning and her friends sat together in the meadow tending their flocks. Black Dog, the medium-sized faithful mutt that helped Bright Morning tend her sheep, was her constant companion, warning if the ewes and ram had gone astray.

One morning, Black Dog barked a sharp warning unlike any other. The girls looked up just in time to see men in tall hats with rifles slung over their shoulders come trotting up on their silver-bridled horses—Spanish slavers!

The girls fled, having no choice but to abandon their flocks. Bright Morning and her friend Running Bird were closest to the evil men and couldn't run fast enough to elude their whirling lariats and galloping mounts!

In moments, the two Navajo maidens were tossed atop the extra horses, their hands bound in front of them. They knew few girls ever managed to escape.

Before Black Dog, far faster than the girls who had escaped, could run off and alert the village, he was clubbed with the butt of a rifle. Led away on a horse, terrified but silent, Bright Morning looked back one last time.

Heather adds various forms of illustrated commentary and sidebars to her summary of the story.

Understanding Inferencing
and Other Skills With Comics

I always have at least some students who are comic book or graphic novel/manga fans. Using comics in the classroom allows them to use a literacy resource from their lives and also provides an opportunity for them to share their expertise with others. Kids often don't understand the complexity of what they need to do as readers. A constant focus on decoding oversimplifies reading and may lead kids away from complex reading strategies like inferencing. Texts like comics make the necessity of these strategies obvious, with their breaks between panels, which are inferencing gaps known as "gutters."

There are now many sophisticated comic books that teach complex content-area concepts from economics, mathematics, science, and history. A quick browse of your local bookstore or Amazon.com can give you plenty of texts to use. Japanese comics, or manga, a current craze among middle schoolers, often use few words and incredible renderings of action and setting to tell stories. All of these comics can be used in a variety of creative ways, as described below.

Teaching Inferencing

The gutters, or spaces between comic panels, are in fact very concrete examples of "inference gaps." Readers must provide the transitions or missing information between the panels to create a coherent text. Comics can therefore be used to help students understand Umberto Eco's notion that in any kind of reading, the author provides us with point A and point E, and it is up to us to take "inferential walks" that lead us from A, creating for ourselves points B, C, and D to make sure we end up at point E in a way that makes coherent sense.

When we look at comics together, I ask my students to describe the panel-to-panel action. As they "fill in the gutter," offering plot points and other details that are not shown, I ask them to justify their elaborations. Another technique is to copy comics with a panel missing, and ask students to supply the action in the missing panel. This variation allows students to see how different authorial choices lead to different meanings. Students can then compose comics together or alone in ways that leave inference gaps for readers and that develop many other capacities that transfer to understanding multimodal literacies and textual conventions and structures in general (see Frey & Fisher, 2004; Hughes, King, Perkins, & Fuke, 2011).

Teaching Text-Specific (Genre) Conventions

Comics generally consist of four panels that correspond to narrative structure: exposition, complication, climax, and resolution/comment/punch line. Students can create comic strips to recapture the sequence of any kind of plot, text structure, or conceptual presentation. In fact, I have not found a text structure, strategy, or text convention that I cannot teach through comics (see Smith and Wilhelm, 2010 for a full discussion). For example, they might follow any of the following structures:

Compare and contrast: The first panel depicts what is being compared and why, the second panel shows similarities, the third panel shows differences, and the fourth offers a conclusion.

Definition: Panel one introduces the term; panel two contains examples of the idea; panel three shows non-examples; panel four offers a definition and uses of the definition.

Summary: Single-panel comics, like those of the famous Far Side, are a kind of tableau that is great for summarizing the central point of a story.

When students are through with such work, they will have a solid introduction to these text-types, how they work, and how the various conventions and parts work together to achieve functional ends. They will have developed the foundational capacities to meet the CCSS requirements to "analyze the structure" of expository texts, including how specific details, moves and structural components "relate to each other and the whole."

Argument structures are also privileged in disciplinary work and by the CCSS:

Basic argument: Successive panels show the claim, a compelling piece of evidence, a warrant, and a conclusion.

Argument of judgment: Claim asserting a judgment on a compelling issue, evidence supporting the judgment, warranting and backing tying the evidence to the claim, response to reservation.

Argument of policy: Claim about a problem and potential solution, evidence of problem, evidence of feasibility of solution, description of the implementation of policy. (for fully described units for teaching various kinds of narrative, expository and argument texts, see Wilhelm, Smith, & Fredricksen, 2012)

When they are through, students will be well on their way to, as the Common Core State Standards require, "Delineate and evaluate [an] argument and specific claims... including the validity of the reasoning [and] the relevance and sufficiency of the evidence."

Script Reading and Writing

Scripts have many conventions that are unique, and this places special challenges on readers and writers of this kind of text. My friend Jamie Heans asks his students to translate comic strips into dramatic scripts before they start to read a play. In this way, they learn about speaker designation, stage directions, setting directions, character directions, and more. All of these are conventions of scripts that do not exist in any other kind of text. Doing this several times helps Jamie's students to understand that when they read a script, they are being prompted to visualize settings and characters, to hear characters speaking, see where they are standing, and perceive what they are doing.

Please note well that in all cases, students are learning to read and understand particular kinds of text structures and related conventions through composing that text structure and using those conventions.

Teaching Symbolism and Irony

Task-specific conventions are those that can be found in any kind of text type but which go well beyond the general processes that are necessary to successfully read any kind of text. Symbolism and irony are examples of such conventions. They are task-specific because they can occur in any kind of genre, and do specific kinds of work no matter what the genre. Readers must recognize the cues that this process must be used to make meaning and must know how to implement the required interpretive operations. This relates to the CCSS standards about recognizing and making use of textual conventions. Comics are particularly good at teaching different forms of symbolism and irony and how to read these forms. Comics are usually meant to be funny and often turn on irony. Kids can also be asked to create cartoons that express various kinds of irony.

We need to help students understand that irony requires us to recognize a literal or expected meaning, and then an implied or alternative meaning that subverts the literal. Michael Smith (1989) explains that the reader of irony needs to understand the literal meaning and recognize that there is an implied alternate meaning by noticing the following tip-offs (from Booth, 1974):

- A straightforward warning that we might need to read carefully or that we shouldn't believe everything we read.

- A speaker in the text proclaims a known error (thereby distancing the author from the speaker).

- There is a conflict between what an individual character thinks and what he says or does. There is a conflict of belief between characters, or a character believes something we find hard to justify.

- There is a clash of style; some information is presented in a different way stylistically.

After noticing any of the above tip-offs, we need to take these four steps:

- Reject the surface meaning.
- Decide what is not under dispute that we can believe.
- Apply our knowledge of the world to generate a reconstructed meaning that makes more sense, replacing what is under dispute with something that makes more sense.
- Check our reconstructed meaning against our knowledge of the world, the author, other books, and so on, as far as we are able. Ask, Does this now make sense?

A comic book summary of a story from Tim O'Brien's collection *The Things They Carried*.

In this Julius Caesar cartoon, the soothsayer proclaims a known error. His drinking also codes him as unreliable. This is an ironic commentary on the play, in which the soothsayer is reliable, but is not believed, and the result is the same.

Floor Plans/Setting

To help students visualize complete settings, have them find or create a map of a setting from a text. I also often ask them to create a floor plan of an important room or setting so that they can be helped to visualize events and interactions in that space. Sometimes we even recreate such an imaginary space in our classroom.

Creating floor plans and room maps can help the reader visualize scenes and move imaginatively through these "story spaces."

Photo Scavenger Hunt

Teacher Brooke Merow provides students with digital cameras and sets them off on scavenger hunts to find settings, images, visual patterns, and situations that parallel elements from a story they are reading.

For example, when studying repetition and parallelism, Brooke asked students to bring in repeated and parallel images. They discussed the effects of this kind of imaging, and then talked about how this technique is also used in writing. When studying contrast and juxtaposition, she asked them to take or find pictures in which very different shapes or figures were contrasted. Again, effects and parallel writing techniques were discussed.

Student photographs can be used to teach about the effect of various constructions like compare-contrast.

Story Collages

Teacher Jane Chamberlain uses story collages to prompt students to attend to particular story elements like major characters, significant events, and settings. But she also often prompts them to include important details or motifs, the author's meaning, the reader's response to the story, something the reader visualized that was not explicitly stated, or a visual relating the text to another text from the unit they are engaged in. Many of these prompts assist students with inferencing and all of them assist in meeting specific standards in the CCSS.

Because it can often imply something deep and abstract through the concrete and superficial, poetry is considered condensed, imagistic, nuanced, and referential.

Perhaps because of this, my students often have great difficulty reading and understanding poetry. After a visit to a neighboring school, however, one of them—Becky (one of many instances in my career when a student suggested a teaching intervention to me)—came up with a helpful idea for understanding poems. Her idea was to make poetry collages, which can be used to do several different things. Students can be asked to create each image suggested by the poem or an image for each line or section. Or they might create a collage of images directly suggested by the poem on the left side of a posterboard, put the poem itself in the middle, and then make a collage of their response on the right. Their responses might include what they construe to be the implied, or deep meaning, of the poem, a personal response, or information about a current world situation that the poem prompts them to consider.

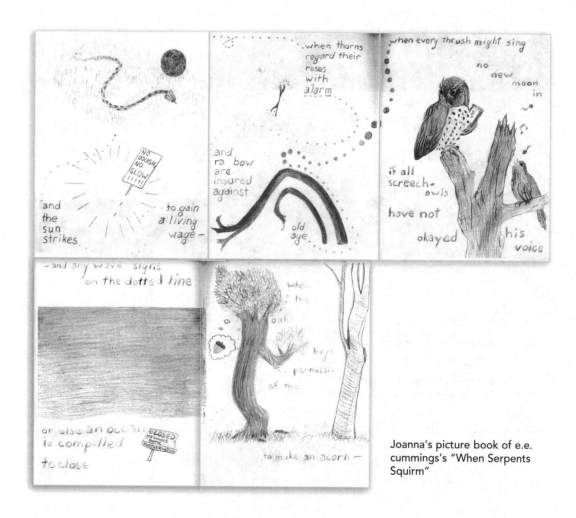

Joanna's picture book of e.e. cummings's "When Serpents Squirm"

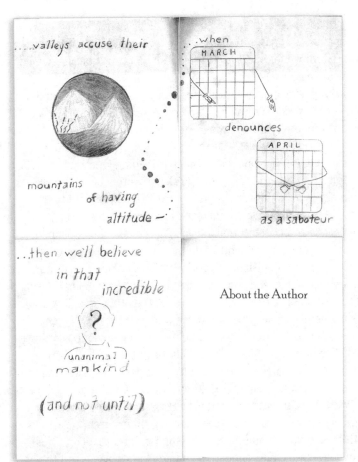

...valleys accuse their

mountains
of having
altitude –

...then we'll believe
in that
incredible

?

unanimal
mankind

(and not until)

...when

MARCH

denounces

APRIL

as a saboteur

About the Author

More of Joanna's
picture book.

Bringing Life to Literature

The techniques explored in this chapter are meant to assist students to visualize the landscape of character, action, event, and situation. They also promote multimodal literacies in general, and an understanding of text structures and conventions in particular, as well as how these contribute to creating and expressing meanings. But because of the very nature of reading as a transactional pursuit in which we bring our own needs, questions, and experiences to bear in conversation with a text, these techniques also prompt students to bring their life experience to their meaning-making conversations with a text. This stimulates students to make inferences and to begin searching for deeper implied meanings that reside in the textual conversation.

CCSS

Anchor Standards
for Reading, 3–9

These techniques also encourage students to mark and display their own identity and values, often in relationship or opposition to a text. This is something students, like all human beings, desire and value. But it is also something that is typically denied them in school (Smith & Wilhelm, 2002).

One of the most beautiful poetry collages I have ever seen was my seventh grade student Tanya's poster of Shel Silverstein's poem "This Bridge Will Take You Half Way There." (The poster was unfortunately thrown away by an overzealous custodian.) Tanya created half a beautiful bridge made of wild scaffolds. This, she explained, was "the text the author offers to me. It gets you started on your reading journey." In the center of the poster, poised on the end of the bridge as if it were a diving board overhanging the abyss was a picture of herself, poised to dive. Thought bubbles emanated from her head, the ones closest to her imagined the rest of the bridge, using various different materials and construction ideas. "This is me," she explained, "imagining how I want to finish the story, which I have to do, because the text only 'takes you half way there.' You have to finish it on your own. I'm thinking the author wants me to finish the bridge using his own construction ideas, but I am going to bring my own ideas, so even though the bridge will take me over to the other side, it will do so in the way that fits my needs, to help me see 'those wonderful worlds' I want to see." On the far right side of the poster were thought bubbles of the imagined settings and events Tanya wanted to experience. "The story is half the author's," she claimed, "and half mine. We make it together." I was astounded! It was a perfect demonstration and explanation of transactional reader response theory from a seventh grader!

Tanya captures a powerful argument for using visual strategies. All of the techniques explored here can be used to help students bring themselves to texts, to stake their own identities and values, and to not only understand texts and the authors behind them, but to embrace and oppose them in different ways, and to build on texts to create connections to themselves and the world they live in and want to live in. Reading is not a powerful and transformative pursuit if it is conceived of in terms of decoding and fluency, but it becomes a most wonderful and potent way to transform our capacities, our own inner landscapes and the world itself when it is seen—as it should be—as a set of unconstrained strategies for making meanings that can inform who we are, who we will become, and what can be achieved in our own lives and out in the world.

MOVING PAST MAIN IDEAS
Identifying, Place-holding, and Interpreting Key Ideas to Create Knowledge

Sometimes even the most unreflective teacher is taught a lesson that can't be shrugged off. Such lessons are an open invitation to reflect and transform one's teaching. It happened to me most memorably during a miserable year that had fallen on me like a ton of bricks. During that year I spent a lot of extra time in the shower, contemplating taking sick days and switching professions.

I'd been sent from the high school to the middle school to teach a load including two classes of eighth-grade remedial reading. Initially I thought it was a demotion—that I had been sent "down" to the middle school. In retrospect, it was the best thing that ever happened to me as a teacher. But I still imagine that first year as a series of Batman sounds: YOW! and KAPOW! and OOFF! I was simply getting beaten up.

The problem was that my students resisted everything. One of them, Danny, told me: "I ain't never read, I ain't never going to read, and you can't make me." A few kids did actually cooperate perfunctorily with a lesson or two, but there was no real substantive engagement. Most of my students refused to do anything, while many actively resisted, telling me how stupid each assignment was: "This is boring." "This is crap!" "How is this going to help us?"

I tried behavior programs, detentions, lectured them on responsibility, provided rewards and punishments galore—all techniques befitting a curriculum-centered, behavioristic approach (Kohn, 1996). Out of desperation, I began to experiment wildly. For the first time, I did some pre-assessments and interest inventories: I began interviewing kids about their school and reading experiences. I asked them directly why they hated school and reading and my class so much. In fact, this was the beginning of my journey as a teacher researcher, only I didn't know it. All I knew is that I was stunned by their answers. They gave me a glimmer of understanding that my students might be right, that the activities I assigned were not connected to their current needs—as readers or people - or the realities of their foreseeable futures.

Still desperate, I chose new materials and we started reading magazines, children's books, and young adult literature about topics "closer to home." This was the first time I used S. E. Hinton's *The Outsiders* and *That Was Then, This Is Now*. Though certainly not unqualified successes, they were my most engaging units. I began to think systematically about what seemed to work and what didn't, what students would resist and what they would try. I asked them to help me, and some of them did. Others, like Tricia, would respond to each request with the comment, "You are such a loser!"

Even after making a little progress, I was still demoralized. But I realized that the kids were even more demoralized, and that while I had some power to help them, they had little power to help me or themselves. They were caught in a system that did not work or make sense for them.

Starting From Scratch

The next year, I jumped at the chance to join an integrated teaching team. It had to be better than what I'd just been through. The team was organized as the EEN house (Exceptional Educational Needs) and we had all of the labeled kids (LD, ED, ADHD, ESL, LFS) in a mainstreamed situation. Our job was to find a way to usefully teach all of the students together.

With this group, my education as a teacher continued. I had learned to listen to kids, and I found some great colleagues. The one to whom I owe more than I can say is Paul Friedemann, who became my team teaching partner for six years in the EEN house. He helped me think through things, and he always had the energy and vision to want to try something new to solve the myriad problems that came up. When something didn't go well, he'd say, "Jeff, let's change it! We have the power!" Paul has the consummate teacher-researcher attitude: "If something is broken, let's fix it. If something is going well, let's make it even better."

We struggled together, and at the end of the first year, Paul told me that he was ready to start from scratch. "School doesn't make sense to these kids! Our classes don't make sense," he told me. "We have to redo things so they make sense to the kids or we will never get anywhere!"

So we agreed to rethink everything—our purposes, our theories, our assignments, our techniques, even our schedule (we shared the same kids for five periods and ended up blocking our classes together in a school where this was unique). At the same time, I was taking classes at the University of Wisconsin from Rich Lehrer, a leading cognitive scientist. Rich was tremendously helpful to us and generous with his time. He is also a proponent of "learning by inquiry and design" (Lehrer, 1993; Wilhelm, 2007) and "understanding by design" (Wiggins & McTighe, 2001). Both of these teaching models are based squarely on the sociocultural learning-centered theory.

Paul and I decided to try the inquiry frame for teaching. We superimposed it over the curriculum we were required to teach, basically addressing the same material by reorganizing it into integrated themes and reframing it with a new orientation and purpose. We were surprised at how all the essential ideas we had been covering in a curriculum-centered way actually fit into inquiry themes that allowed student activity to be purposeful—allowing them to be active in achieving deep foundational understandings.

Our attempt started off slow, with an initial five-day unit on designing personality profiles on hyperstacks for a unit on personal identity. Throughout the next couple of years, we corresponded constantly with Rich Lehrer, and he visited our school several times. Three years later, everything we did was inquiry driven, organized around four quarter-long inquiry units that addressed all the designated curriculum material. Our students were thriving, and we were enjoying them and each other. Hey, even test scores were going up. Life was good—very good—for both of us and much more important—for our students, even the ones who had previously struggled.

Becoming Authors of Knowledge

This book has been about using visuals to create meaning in concert with textual information and data. Now it moves on to discussing visuals to place-hold information so that it can be operated on—added to, analyzed, critiqued, and used. Previous chapters were about fleshing out and enlivening textual information by using visuals to help students transact with the text. I shared many techniques that can be used to frame a purposeful inquiry context (frontloading), and that will help students discern and place-hold the information offered in a text (tableaux, timelines, the central focus sequence). In this chapter, I offer some further techniques for discerning the main ideas of particular texts through the use of visual tools. But I do so in the context of inquiry, of helping students to see various patterns and perspectives across texts and situations, so that deep understandings can be achieved. I move to helping students to operate on and interpret visually represented information for the purpose of analyzing and using what has been learned. And finally, I show how visuals can be used as the media for "authoring" and "designing" knowledge, as students represent what they are learning and have learned.

Rich Lehrer's research into classroom inquiry demonstrates that teachers tend to misunderstand the notion of "inquiry." Instead of being a rigorous induction into disciplinary knowledge and ways of knowing, most of what is called "inquiry" simply involves student discovery or even copying information from sources. As a result, it often produces facile understanding and even plagiarism. Further, the end point is usually a simple report or project, not the use, application, or extension of information. In true inquiry, students cannot plagiarize because the point is not to recapitulate information; the point is to go beyond what is currently known and to create a unique and usable "knowledge artifact." Such learning is problem-based. Problems animate our learning in the world because we must use the knowledge we gain by making a decision or taking action to solve real issues. In problem solving, students must know the various perspectives about an issue and then choose, adapt, and develop new ways of using these perspectives.

The concept of "usability" is important to David Perkins's notion of "knowledge," which he differentiates from "information" (1991). In the chart on the next page, I differentiate the concepts of information and knowledge. Perkins (1991) posits that knowledge is distinguished by structuredness, systematicity, applicability, and extensibility. Information does not share any of these features. Based on recent advances in cognitive psychology and literacy, I've added some additional contrasts between information and knowledge in the chart on the next page.

Information	Knowledge
is received from outside sources.	is socially and culturally constructed; must involve personal effort, contributions, and connection-making to be internalized by an individual.
may not involve a mental model.	involves creating a new mental model (to the learner) for understanding a concept, process, or genre.
is usually decontextualized; taught separately from use.	is always contextualized—learned and applied in a situation in which the knowledge is required and used.
is recapitulated.	is transformed, transmediated, re-represented in new ways.
is submitted or sometimes displayed (e.g., homework).	is usable over time by self and others; can be adapted and transferred to new situations.
is "schoolish"—only counts in school contexts.	is "toolish"—can help to perform tasks and extend human abilities in the world outside of school.
is completed and then discarded (e.g., term papers, tests).	is archival and extensible over time, by creator and others; can be continually revised and built upon.
is fragmented.	is structured and systematic—there is a clear relationship and interplay between structure, details, and use.
is linear.	is weblike—data is interconnected within and across sources, like Internet hotlinks.
is established, inert, static.	is generative, additive, dynamic, evolving, revisable.
is accepted, unjustified.	is justified—reasoning is made visible and accountable—and reservations are acknowledged and responded to.
is considered to be "factual."	is considered to be socially constructed and therefore revisable, extensible, and so on.

Throughout this chapter, I attempt to show how the visual strategies recommended throughout the whole of this book are forms of knowledge construction and representation rather than ways to merely purvey "factual" information. The process of reading, finding relevant information, seeing connections and patterns across information sources, developing missing information, and shaping the accrued knowledge into usable knowledge artifacts is the very process of inquiry and designing knowledge. This chapter focuses on using visuals to find, place-hold, and analyze major ideas. In the end, students should be able to see with,

think with, and use these major ideas in ways consistent with higher order thinking, disciplinary work, and the CCSS.

Picture Mapping

After Reading:
Picture Mapping

Anchor Standards
for Reading, 1–9
Multimodal
Complexity

One of the most versatile visualization techniques I've ever used is picture mapping, an idea I learned 20 years ago from the CRISS Project (Content Reading in Secondary Schools). Basic picture mapping involves identifying and summarizing in pictures (icons, indices that suggest an idea, or symbols) the key ideas of a textual passage. To bring picture mapping in line with how readers identify key details and add together their meanings, I've added the requirements that students identify the topic and create a pictorial topic representation. I also ask that they consider the meaning that accrues from the relationships between the details to come up with a central focus/main idea that they also represent visually. The picture map then provides a powerful visual summary of how a text explored and commented on the topic (i.e., the general subject all the key details address).

An essential element of text comprehension is understanding how ideas are patterned throughout a text. There are six basic ways in which text details are organized to create meaning through their relationships:

Stated relationships. Authors identify the relationship between details—for example, in *Roll of Thunder*, that Mr. Morrison's huge size was caused by white slave owner's breeding the biggest slaves together over the course of generations.

Simple implied relationships. Authors put related ideas close together in a text, assuming that readers will see the connections—for example, that Cassie's beating of Lillian Jean was on her body, not her face, because of warnings Papa had given her earlier in the book.

Complex implied relationships. These are more challenging patterns of meaning in which the reader is asked to infer the meaning of details far apart from each other and stretched across a text. These may include textual gaps that the author expects readers to be able to fill in. For example, in *Roll of Thunder*, consider what happens between Uncle Hammer and Mr. Morrison in Uncle Hammer's car. Readers are given the initial details of Uncle Hammer's resolve to confront Charlie Simms (that would certainly end in a lynching), and the details of their return home the next morning. We must infer from the available details that Mr. Morrison must have talked Uncle Hammer out of going to the Simmses.

4 **Authorial generalization.** This is the point made by the accumulated relationships of details throughout a text—for example, in *Roll of Thunder* the results of fighting injustice in various ways show that using your intelligence to fight, in subtle ways using the law and the existing system, is more effective than direct assaults through physical force or the use of emotions.

5 **Local text structure patterns.** These are patterns for organizing details that are embedded into a text at a local level. Such structural patterns include simple listing, time order (chronology), cause and effect, compare and contrast, classification, and definition.

6 **Global/genre and text structure patterns.** These are superstructure patterns that organize a whole text, give it coherence, and provide an overall road map for reading. Some of the same patterns that work locally can also organize a whole text—for example, compare and contrast, classification, extended definition, and narrative chronology. Other generic superstructure patterns include argument, ironic monologue, fable, and dramatic script.

Basic Picture Mapping Directions

Have students work in groups of three or four to complete a picture map. This group size is small enough so that everyone will be involved but large enough that there will be an exchange of ideas and discussion. Instruct groups to:

1 **Read through the text excerpt.**

2 **Identify the topic of the reading** (the general subject that all major ideas or events share in common) and create a pictorial representation of it.

3 **Go through the text and mark or list each key idea about the topic, paying attention to the key detail clues including:**

- First and last sentences of the text because introductions and conclusions often signal the topic and key ideas about it

- Paragraph breaks, which often signal a new key idea

- First and last sentences of paragraphs

- Highlights, boldface, italics, bullets, boxes, and font changes, all of which signal attention to key ideas

- Quoted material

- Surprises, shifts, and changes in focus, direction, or emphasis

4 **Consider how to represent or symbolize each key idea with a picture or symbol**—as simply and clearly as possible.

5 **Identify how the key details work together to create a deep meaning and statement about the world outside the text.** This is the central focus statement (also known as a main idea or thematic generalization). Consider how to represent this main idea in a single picture.

I often have students initial their contributions to the completed map or identify their contributions in writing on the back of the map. This adds one more layer of individual accountability. When these projects are complete, students want to share and present them to each other, and I typically have them do so, as well as having them post their picture map in the classroom.

Advanced Picture Mapping Ideas

- Add to each key detail picture a sticky note describing how you knew that each key detail was essential and didn't just provide texture.

- Demonstrate several key ideas with one picture or symbol.

- Show the patterns and connections between ideas or progressions of ideas if the organization and structure of the text are important to the point it expresses (e.g., organize the picture map into a timeline if there is historical cause and effect, into a family tree if it involves relationships or classes of information, Venn diagram if it involves definition or compare-contrast).

- Add a response corner (could also be done on the back of the picture map) depicting your response to the text and your feelings about the information presented and issues raised. Indicate what surprised you, what you want to do as a result of this reading, and so on. You could even draw a picture of yourself thinking about the text, showing to what degree you accept, would adapt, or resist the message and implications for thinking and living provided by the text. If several of you worked on the picture map together, you could each use a corner for your individual responses.

- Use a picture map to summarize the whole unit. Be sure to show the key details across various texts and experiences, how they relate to each other, and the conclusion (big understandings/central foci) you gleaned from the unit as a whole.

- Show your picture map to another group. Let them guess what each symbol/picture and the various placements/relationships mean.

- Use your picture map to show students in other groups what was important about your text. If individuals or groups are reading different texts for the same inquiry unit, make sure your picture map is strong enough that they will know the most important things you leaned about the inquiry topic so they can think with these ideas, too.

- Use your picture map to study for a test, write a paper, or just to jog your memory. Discuss how it helps to meet these purposes.

- Hang the picture maps in the classroom and use them as references for writing assignments, tests, and discussions.

Picture maps provide a powerful visual summary of the topic (what all the key details have in common), the key details themselves, the structured relationships of these ideas, and the central focus. The process of creating them helps students to deeply understand how text structures work to develop and express particular meanings. Understanding this as a reader aids students to organize texts as writers (Hillocks, 1986).

Picture Mapping Adaptations

Often the thematic meaning of a story, or even a history, hinges on how a situation or a character is changed by the events in the narrative. In this case, a Before and After picture map allows students to analyze and see the patterns of change, so that they can draw conclusions about general principles of being and acting in the world. Cause-and-effect relationships can be added by connecting before and after values of a character through a map. For example, I recently had students depict the changes in Eustace from C. S. Lewis's *The Voyage of the Dawn Treader* that result from the challenges, adventures, and relationships he experiences on his epic voyage. Some students wrote a series of several postcards to create a character-change postcard sequence, which depicted the gradual changes Eustace undergoes and how these changes are related to various experiences.

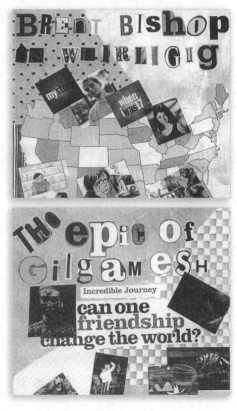

Flow or step charts often work nicely to depict cause and effect, narrative, or process description. In a flow chart, students show how ideas and events relate to each other over time. These can also be extended through the use of mirror mapping techniques, in which students compare and contrast anything through a map (e.g., perspectives). Students might compare their own and an author's or character's values at different points in a story.

For example, teacher Cindy Dean has her students create flow charts of the hero quest archetype during an extended unit in which her students ask, "What is a hero?" and explore structures such as the archetype. She has students create mirror maps comparing archetypal mythological heroes to heroes of today.

A poetry collage comparing the quests of Brent Bishop and Gilgamesh.

Students are expected to show how both the mythological and contemporary heroes share aspects of the archetype, including a sequestered childhood, a special teacher, a loyal sidekick, a special but hidden skill, the undertaking of a challenge that involves a quest, a descent into the underworld or a spiritual encounter, and the aiding of others who benefit from the successful completion of the quest.

Past-Present-Future Triptych

Cindy also adapts the self-text-world triptych concept so that students can examine cause-and-effect influences on characters, events, policies, and proposals. One panel of the triptych designates an event or quality that was exhibited before the story, the middle panel depicts the current situation, and the final panel shows future events, including possible consequences or possibilities now opened.

Flashback Mapping

In this activity, students compare current events to those in a story about the past. Paul Fleischman's *Dateline Troy*, in which he compares the events of the Trojan War to analogous modern historical events, can prove an inspiring model for this technique.

Fleischman compares current events to those from the Trojan War.

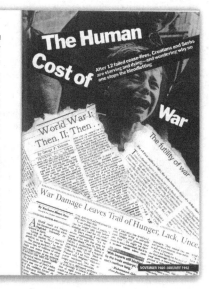

Students could depict a mythological event on one page and a corresponding modern-day event on the facing page, as Fleishman does, or even create an extended picture book or hypermedia book that connects a succession of various story events with various modern ones.

Such techniques can be effective any time you want students to make text-to-text connections or to see points of contact or analogies between different stories (e.g., between the YA novel *America* and *Great Expectations*), different phenomena (freezing and rigor mortis), different processes (cleaning your house and fasting's effect on the body or growing up in a family and being a colony).

How These Techniques Spark Transformative Discussions

As I walk around while students create picture maps, I always hear similar discussions. Students are intensely discussing what the topic might be and how precisely they can identify and represent it. They argue about key details—which ones are important and which are merely texture. The students help each other to see the patterns of relationships among the details, to discern the trajectory and flow of ideas through a piece, and to highlight examples of these key details.

In particular, they passionately consider the central focus statement. Students always talk at length about how to represent the ideas. For David Quammen's "Republic of Cockroaches," they ask "Is this really about cockroaches, or something else that they represent? Like survival, or how species adapt?" "What is the nuclear radiation sign?" "How can we show that cockroaches will eat anything but cucumbers?" "How can we show the cockroach is the oldest creature on the planet?"

These discussions about representing written ideas in visual form involve what semiotic theoreticians call "transmediation." These theorists argue that we create and demonstrate deep understanding by our ability to put ideas into a different form—by putting a written text or picture into our own words; creating a dance or movement expression of a process; or, in this case, putting written text into patterns of visual representations. The power of visual display is often wrapped up in the power of transmediation to transform ideas from information into knowledge. This transformation makes these ideas personally constructed, systematic, structured, extensible, and usable artifacts that we can think and work with.

One of my seventh graders once described his own process of transmediation to his picture mapping group. I'm paraphrasing here, but it was a chant that went

A picture map for David Quammen's "Republic of Cockroaches."

something like this: "First we have to read it! Then we have to talk it! Then we have to draw it! Then we have to organize it! Then we have to use it! Then we have to share it!"

This is entirely in keeping with Vygotskian ideas about learning. First, all learning is metaphoric, and the new must be connected to the already known; it must be operated on, connected, and transformed into something usable by the learner. Second, for new ideas to be deeply understood, they must be considered from all sides, in all dimensions, and from various perspectives.

There are many other ways of transmediating texts by transforming them into other forms—making excerpts into wordless books, fable books, flip books, comic books, hypermedia animations, twisted fairy tales, timelines, flow charts, videos, and more. These are not simple projects; they are devices that encourage and demonstrate deep understanding.

Quote Books

I enjoy having students create quote books, asking them to collect the most important, revealing quotations from a particular character. I then ask them to create a book of these quotations, including illustrations of their meaning and explanations of their significance.

To get at repeated motifs, themes, and authorial generalizations, this can also be done for a historical figure. For example, I just finished reading David McCullough's Pulitzer Prize–winning biography of John Adams. I was so impressed with John Adams that I went back through the book and pulled out my favorite quotations from his speeches, diaries, and correspondence. Reading these quotes over gave me a great sense of his stance toward life and helped me to know him better in both a personal way and a historical way. I could easily have added visuals to create a quotations book.

The same thing could be done for an author, a character, for one text, or across texts. One of my seventh-grade students, Cora, created a book of quotations across the many books she had read by Katherine Paterson. She grouped the quotations around central themes that she discerned in Paterson's work, like the importance of relationship, forgiveness, and dealing with death and loss.

Take-offs on quotations books include passage displays, in which a student or students make a poster of the meaning of an important passage from a text or a directly stated central focus. The quoted passage can be the center of the display or pleased artistically in various ways (broken up into parts or repeated) through the artistic display.

Quotations/Poems on the Subway

I noticed while riding on the subway that on each car one of the advertising panels was an illustrated line or two from a poem or a quotation from a literary/historical character. (I later discovered it is a campaign in many major U.S. cities called Poetry in Motion, sponsored by Barnes and Noble.) I brought the idea back to school and had my students create illustrated quotations or poems for the hallway in our school. Several of my male students took to posting limericks above all the school urinals. They called it "Poetry in the Can." Hey, whatever works!

A Quote Book from Maya Angelou's *I Know Why the Caged Bird Sings*.

Visual Correspondence

In this response activity I ask students to write a postcard or letter exchange between characters or historical figures from textual material they have read. The correspondence must review important information, give personal perspectives on the information and its importance, demonstrate relationships among the characters or historical figures who are corresponding, and perhaps even provide elaborations on the information.

These postcards and letters can be

- from a character (or group of characters) in one text to a character in another one.

- between two characters from the same text.

- between minor and major characters.

- between unmentioned imaginary characters and characters who might have had an influence on them (an American patriot and King George III, for example).

- from real people to characters and vice versa.

- from you to a character or vice versa.

The postcards require students to imagine an event, setting, or scene and then to communicate their perspective, in role, about this scene to another character. Then the receiver must write back. Sometimes kids write both cards; other times I have them exchange, actually responding in role to another student's postcard. If students exchange letters, I might require them to use visuals through a correspondence poster by posting the two letters on a posterboard, designing appropriate stationery, and illustrating the area around the letters with scenes and events that are described. Or students could provide visual enclosures that are appropriate to their correspondence, such as maps, photographs, drawings, and journal pages.

From "The Day They Stopped the War." A student in character as Major Cartwright from England writes a postcard to a German officer about their men's Christmas day soccer match.

As you could see from the front, this is a very disgraceful time. But unfortunately it was the only time there was peace. I don't know how but these men were able to make peace on Christmas day and the Pope couldn't even do it. It all must be part of Christmas miracles. Too bad it didn't last so everyone would stop the war. Write to me some time after the war. If we live that long.

Hope the war ends soon,
Major Cartwright

From *Voyage of the Dawn Treader*

Dear Peter,
Narnia is just as I remembered it! Reepicheep, head of the talking mice, is on board! Also is Caspian! As you see on the cover is a picture of what we are sailing into. If the sun looks large to you it is not because I never got around to drawing lessons but because it is larger! Also the water is fresh! We draw it up by the bucket full and drink it, it tastes indescribable! We do not get hungry or tired. Eustace is a brick!. He has shaped up after being turned into a dragon. He's quite enjoyable and liked by all. I must go on the poop.   Your Sister,
                                                              Lucy

More Ways to Highlight Key Details or Themes

There are many other ideas for highlighting the key details or main ideas in a text. Several teachers I know have students create symbolic borders or picture frames for the visuals they create. These symbolic borders can communicate the meaning of the scene that is depicted, various perspectives on it, the reader's personal response to it, self-world-intra- or intertextual connections to the presented information, uses for the information, and so on.

Response Mapping

Another kind of pattern that is useful to track, place-hold, and study is that of the individual reader's response (or the response of groups of readers). Students, as kids and as humans, are intensely self-interested. It is interesting, fun, and useful for them to map out their various responses to a text or a series of texts. This, in turn, can serve as a useful springboard for personal exploration and goal setting, as they try new strategies for sharing responses with each other and deepening understanding of texts.

In Phyllis Whitin's excellent book *Sketching Stories, Stretching Minds*, she has students draw pictures of how they read and respond to texts, like mazes or puzzles they were trying to solve, and to use line or pie graphs to summarize the emotional intensity, intellectual engagement, and other features of their response to various parts of the text. Whitin also has students draw their reading and writing processes to study how they work and how they might work more effectively. Students can also be prompted to draw parts of a text that are most interesting, scariest, most uplifting, or most thought provoking.

Learning/Reading Biographies

I have often had my students create visual reading autobiographies that identify the kind of readers they were at various points in their lives by showing what they read, how they read these things, and how they used and shared their reading. Students identify events, books, or situations that affected their attitudes and abilities as readers. These autobiographies can take many forms: pop-up books, picture books, graphic novels, flow charts, or timelines. This project represents a form of personal inquiry into students' own learning processes, and it often lets me understand them in ways that helps me to teach them.

I could share many pages more of visualization ideas, but I imagine you have enough to get immersed in this set of techniques. It's your turn to develop activities of your own! To that end, on the next page I provide guidelines for doing just that.

A scene from Kristy Heller's learning biography in which she explores how she came to detest spelling tests.

Considerations for Teachers Designing a Visualization Tool Activity

When designing visual activities, please demonstrate your understanding of how readers read and respond to literature and other texts and how they "bring meaning forward," learning text by text and activity by activity.

- Each activity should require students to enter and evoke the world of the text.

- The activities should encourage students to elaborate on the text world, to fill in gaps, to make inferences, and to extend their reading to making connections beyond the text.

- The activities should encourage students to revisit textual details and experiences and to reorganize, bring forward, and reflect upon what they have learned.

- The activities should encourage students to achieve a richer and more "valid" reading of the text—to respectfully attend to and consider all relevant textual details even as they operate on these to make personally significant meanings.

- The activities should ask students to hone other skills and develop knowledge outside the domain of the text—for example, learn about interviewing skills, news show formats, review writing, and so on.

- The activities should be fun for the kids and should ask them to learn something they don't already know (instead of just revisiting what they already know) extend understanding and to achieve or practice some new learning processes they have not already mastered.

- The activities should provide some real-world work; pursuing and completing them should help to teach kids in the class about each other and about the book or unit topic; they should be part of a community service or partner school project; and so on. In any case, the work should be real, have some real-world audiences, and do some kind of "social work."

- Please display your knowledge of how visual tools can work as a means to assist students' learning performances.

CHAPTER 12

VISUALIZATION, FORMATIVE ASSESSMENT, AND REFLECTIVE TEACHING

Learning From Students
How to Best Teach Them

The new CCSS for text complexity are startling in their rigor. All students, no matter if they struggle, or their background, or their label from LD to ELL to LFS, will be required to develop the capacity to read college level and career-oriented texts. I wish the CCSS had included "citizenship readiness" with career and college readiness, but this is a goal I can endeavor to meet in my own classroom.

There is only one way to meet these new standards for text complexity, as well as the other rigorous procedural standards and that is to start where students are, and then help them to outgrow themselves as readers,

Q&A 5: How can visualization strategies help prepare students for standardized tests?

learners, and people. Use their preexisting interests and capacities as resources. Begin with students' ZPDs and work forward from there, upping the ante to equip students to read more complex texts by helping them create a repertoire of reading strategies that can be brought forward and made deeper and more complex over time.

It will do no good merely to assign harder texts. Students must be helped, over time and in different ways, to develop the interest, engagement, and deep expertise to fulfill the standards. This will require teachers to differentiate instruction in terms of materials, methods, motivations, group structures, culminating projects, ongoing formative assessments, and more. In turn, this means teachers will need to become very adept at coming to know their students as readers, writers, and learners. They will need to become expert at daily formative assessments that help students name what they know and to help teachers learn about their students and how to best teach them. The prerequisite to this kind of daily meaningful instruction and differentiation is formative assessment, which is an informal kind of continuous teacher research and reflection. This may sound like a lot of extra work, and it can be for teachers practicing in the mechanistic information-transmission mode. But it will be relatively easy and oh-so friendly and rewarding for teachers who are reflective practitioners working within a relational inquiry context with their students.

Teaching With Visual Differentiation

For example, in my latest teaching iterations of *Romeo and Juliet* (which I calculate having taught over 26 of the past 30 years!), I reframed the unit from a textual study of the play into an inquiry into an existential question: "What makes and breaks relationships?" In the latest iteration, I was well familiar with my students' strengths and weaknesses through the daily use of "deliverables" that provided formative assessment (information about what the students could and could not yet do, what they had understood and what they were struggling with). I knew that two of my students were girls from Sudan, via a Kenyan refugee camp, and I knew quite a bit about their lives and their culture. I knew something about the lives and literacy of two boys recently off the boat from Bosnia based on think-aloud activities and other assignments that provided immediate data about their interests, as well as what they knew and could do, and therefore what was possible and appropriate for them to learn next.

If I were teaching a textual study of *Romeo and Juliet* (as I had done many times), I would have been sunk. But fortunately, as I was inquiring with my students into the stated problem: "What makes and breaks relationships?" the playing field was leveled. I certainly knew things that pertained to this inquiry that my students did not. But they knew many things I did not and were asked to bring these to the table of our joint inquiry. They could no longer play "guess what the teacher already knows" because, though I know something about relationships, I do not know the answer to this inquiry question. And far from being marginalized for being from a different culture, or for their relative lack of facility with the English language, my ELLs and LFS students became resources for the rest of the class—their very difference meant they knew things and could lend perspectives that the rest of us lacked. I was reminded of John Dewey's (1916) injunction that democracy is not everybody doing the same thing in the same way, but it is "complementarity"—that is, everybody bringing their unique interests, capacities, and perspectives to bear on a common project. Democracy is akin to a great mosaic of nuanced, respectful, complex, and multifarious understandings.

Differentiation, informed by previous formative assessments, commenced immediately. Frontloading for the unit involved students ranking the value they placed on different descriptions of relationships. The scenarios were short. Small groups read and discussed them together, so even the ELL kids were on board. Difference of opinion was valued as we began to record different attitudes and definitions of better and worse relationships, and what promotes or mucks them up. Students participated in completing surveys and did autobiographical writing prompted by survey items. (For a version of the assignments themselves, see Wilhelm, 2007.) A final frontloading activity asked students to bring in a favorite love song and an original "CD cover" of the song that visually represented the theme on one side and a written explanation of their personal connection to that song on the other. The Sudanese girls both sang "promise songs" (and translations) that they had sung to the boys they had been promised to at the age of twelve. Their CD cover illustrations were a formative assessment that allowed me to see how adept they were at expressing theme and explaining how it was expressed, as well as differentiating it from personal connections (all required by the CCSS). The Bosnian boys both chose songs in Bosnian, which they later translated, which expressed themes about the necessity of loyalty to the loved and the beloved's family and friends—something none of the American songs had expressed. These differences were quite provocative, and led to rich discussions about the costs and benefits of arranged marriages, the need for cultural support for relationships, how personal relationships are parts of larger networks of relationships, and much else.

Because I knew, from prior formative assessments, that many of my students in this regular track class would struggle with the original Shakespearean language from Late Middle English, I asked each student to choose a graphic novel version of the play to read. These texts all use the same graphics, but one version is in simple English, one in modern English, and one in Shakespearean English. In all cases, the illustrations assist in making sense of each scene. At the end of two days, every student had successfully read and understood the basic plot of the play and was feeling good and successful. Everyone was on the same playing field and had the background to successfully contribute to future activities.

As we read the play itself, some students read the original, while others read only excerpts, or excerpts of the original and *Shakespeare Made Easy* (a modern translation side by side with the original). We frontloaded our reading of each section by first watching that scene from Zefferelli's *Romeo and Juliet* or Baz Luhrmann's *William Shakespeare's Romeo and Juliet*. Various short activities, like a cartoon version or tableaux drama summarizing the scene were completed in response, providing further assistance and formative assessment about student comprehension and response, and helping me plan the next lesson and how to differentiate it so that everyone continued to be successful, and therefore engaged. (Sherry Turkle at MIT has shown how puzzles and problem-solving tasks have "natural holding power" as long as participants feel that they are making progress in being successful on the task.)

Students who did not read the whole original text had other readings to do. For example, the Bosnian boys were asked to find a folktale from Bosnia that was a version of *Romeo and Juliet* or at least about relationships. They did so in one day, telling me, "Meester! Meester! We find TWO Bosnian *Romeo and Juliet*!" In fact, they had found two news stories—in Bosnian, of course—that were near-perfect matches. One was a story of a Christian-Muslim couple who jumped off a bridge together because neither family approved of their relationship. This is *Romeo and Juliet*! The other was about an honor killing that escalated into further honor killings. It had many parallels to *Romeo and Juliet*. The texts being in Bosnian, I asked the boys to translate a summary of each for the class, and to present it to us through a sequence of visual tableaux. All of this required great effort and substantive learning. All tasks were also appropriately in their ZPDs; translating from Bosnian to English, composing summaries in English with visual support, identifying a sequence of events and how to visually display them and their connections, presenting in English to their peers but with visual supports were all doable because the visual techniques provided "environmental assistance" to do a task they would have struggled with or found "frustrational" without that assistance.

Throughout the reading, groups of students working as video production teams rewrote, recast, and filmed their own stagings and versions of various scenes. They added commentary about the significance of each scene, how themes were expressed, and how the scene contributed to the overall experience and meaning of the play (note how many of the CCSS anchor standards were met through this activity!).

Students looked forward to watching each other's work, and all students were fully engaged. In the last two acts, video production teams created a video glossary of literary terms by defining the term, reenacting a scene where the term was a convention that created meaning in that scene, and then making a modern day parallel to how the convention worked in everyday communication. All of this rewards CCSS standards for understanding how textual construction and conventions work to create meaning. (Again, for a fuller description of this project, see Wilhelm, 2007.)

Each of these tasks provided differentiation and required problem solving using heuristics, since the tasks could be successfully completed in any number of ways, ways that allowed students to be imaginative, creative, and express their identity and thinking about various issues that came up, yet still required principled conceptual and procedural knowledge. Each task resulted in a "deliverable" that made learning visible and thus provided formative assessment on student understanding, and this could be revised to correct misconceptions or to deepen understanding. Conceptual and procedural understandings were developed in concert.

Throughout, I was a teacher-researcher into my students' understanding of the play, and their use of appropriate strategies necessary to complete our work (e.g., identifying conventions and how they contributed to meaning at the local and global level of text) at the individual student and group level. More than that, the students were deeply considering how to best relate to others, how to address relationship problems in healthy ways, and much more. They could be said to have been directly developing wisdom and practicing how to use what they were learning in their daily living. I have argued that when we do not teach for such joy, wisdom, and use, we are certainly aiming too low (Wilhelm and Novak, 2011).

I learned, through the daily deliverables, what students understood and could use as resources for more complex activity, and what they needed more help with. Each day, we worked with visualization techniques that supported student reading, composing, and thinking with ever more complexity. I could group students for the next class based on who needed what. Yet we still had a shared large group project (understanding the play, creating videos and the video glossary for each other) and often worked as a whole class. Each day, we practiced procedural understandings foregrounded in the CCSS. Every person in the class was valued as an evolving reader and learner, and every person's personhood as a unique human being was celebrated and brought to bear. Everyone worked appropriately in their own ZPD and made gains towards reading more complex texts with ever-greater capacity.

Here's another thing: Our classroom became more authentically democratic, in ways consistent with Walt Whitman's "Democratic Vistas" and Louise Rosenblatt's *The Reader, the Text, and the Poem*. Full democracy is about more than the "common good" (the founding principle of ancient democracy) and "equal rights" (the founding principle of modern democracy); it actualizes these values but also achieves "complementarity" and "mutual regard." Beyond both the "all for one" of the common good and the "one for all" of government protected rights is an "each for each" in which people learn to see one another for who they are and share life and meaning-making with one another. This is a kind of democracy whose center is not in political administration or economic opportunity, but in education, and in any significant problem-solving work that we do together where we seek to learn from each other, to learn how to learn together, and to "draw one another out" as human beings (Wilhelm and Novak, 2011). Inquiry is a way of incrementally inducting students into this kind of democratic work and living. Now that is teaching worth doing.

Changing Classroom Culture Through Visual Strategies as Formative Assessment/Teacher Research

A theme of this book has been the transformation of the cultures of classrooms and of schooling through the reframing of curriculum into democratic inquiry and through the foregrounding of procedures of learning. It's been further argued that inquiry and the teaching of procedures in meaningful contexts of immediate use is the way to best meet the CCSS, and even more important, to truly engage the interests of students, and to promote "learning how to learn," which is transferable to new situations. Formative assessment with or without visuals is a direct means to assist in transforming classroom cultures in ways that will promote inquiry and procedural learning. Formative assessments are not about grades or external authority, but about supporting learning and developing the internal authority and critical standards of the learner. To truly transform classrooms for the benefit of students and their learning, this use of formative assessment needs to become a central concern of every teacher. In fact, if we adopt inquiry models supported by socio-constructivist theory (as I argue we must) then formative assessment is part and parcel of this process.

There are many forms and techniques of quick visual formative assessments—in fact, any of the techniques in this book can either immediately provide quick hits of usable formative assessment data to the teacher or be tweaked to do so. Visual strategies provide immediate feedback and gut checks for both teachers and students.

See, Think, Wonder

Before Reading: See, Think, Wonder

This is a simple and powerful technique that is great for frontloading a unit or reading in a way that makes visible what students already know and can do. Students are given a photograph, painting, spread from a picture book, or even an artifact that obtains to the unit or reading at hand. Students first individually study the object and list what they "see." They then list what these details make them "think," which gets students to make connections and infer. Finally, they "wonder" and ask questions and make predictions that will develop the continuing impulse to read and learn about the topic. We recently did this with photos from What the World Eats, asking students to compare what they saw, thought and wondered about in photos of what American families ate versus families from Japan, Somalia and other places around the world. This not only activated and built background knowledge, but also generated many questions and wonderings that led us energetically into our initial readings around the inquiry "How does what we eat affect us?"

Concentric Circles

After Reading:
Concentric Circles

This technique is great for making students' growing understanding visible to the student, peers, and teacher. Before the unit begins, students fill out the innermost circle to identify what they already know and think about the essential question. Every few days, students add another circle and write about: what they're thinking now. This shows students how their understanding is evolving and becoming ever more complex over time. It also provides a quick formative assessment to the teacher about what the student thinks is important and what she might have missed. (For more of this kind of formative assessment, see Wilhelm, Wilhelm and Boas, 2009.)

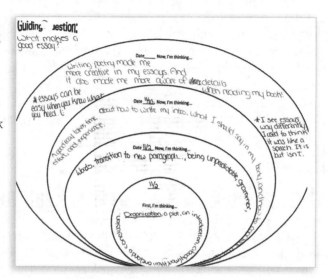

Formative Assessment, the CCSS, and Transformed Instruction

One of my own research methods professors, Beth Graue (1993), has argued that "assessment and instruction are often conceived as curiously separate in both time and purpose" (p. 291, emphasis added). Formative assessment is part of the learning process and abets the purpose of the current inquiry.

The cognitive revolution of the past half-century, outlined in this book, has reintroduced the concept of "mind" to education. In contrast to traditional, mechanistic theories of learning such as information-transmission, we now know that learning is an active, social, multimodal process of mental construction and sense making. We further know that intelligent thought involves metacognition, self-monitoring, and wide-awake awareness about when and how to use various procedures, and that "expertise" develops in a discipline as a principled and coherent way of representing, thinking about, and solving problems, not as an accumulation of mere information.

The takeaway? Deep understanding is based on conceptual and procedural principles, and supports transfer to new problems in new situations. Deep understanding can be made visible, is justified, and is made accountable in actual achievement and application.

Therefore good assessment must be ongoing and formative, moving students incrementally toward greater awareness and expertise. This also means that to evaluate student learning is to evaluate teaching and inform the next steps in teaching. Learning and teaching are seen as flip sides of the same coin. The goal here is to create a learning culture where students and teachers work together, and expect to work together, to figure out how to solve problems in ways that make sense. Further, this redistributes power and establishes more collaborative teacher relationships with and among students. These collaborations are for the purpose of learning, assessing the progress and status of learning, and of informing and assisting the learning that will come next.

Formative Assessment and Evaluation of Teaching

In addition to using assessment to monitor and promote individual students' learning and students learning together, classroom assessments of all kinds should help us to examine, improve, and even invent new knowledge about teaching and teaching principles and practices. The teacher, with the help of students, becomes an inquirer into teaching various processes and concepts, and creates new ways of doing so. This includes all the kinds of formative assessments described here as well as more formal critical action-research studies.

As Shepard (2000) pointedly suggests, "it will be helpful for teachers to make their investigations of teaching visible to students, for example, by discussing with them decisions to redirect instruction, stop for a mini-lesson, and so forth. This seems to be fundamentally important to the idea of transforming the culture of the classroom. If we want to develop a community of learners—where students naturally seek feedback and critique their own work—then it is reasonable that teachers would model this same commitment to using data systematically as it applies to their own role in the teaching and learning process."

It is also reasonable to expect that students and teachers name and celebrate what they have learned, justify this learning, and set the next goals for learning. We will then truly have become a community of learners with a new level of independence and the capacity to solve novel ill-formed problems, the kind that exists so plentifully in the world beyond school.

To Make Learning Visible

B ette Manchester, a wonderful principal with whom I worked for several years would say to her teachers, "Your job is to create perceived competencies and perceived autonomy, and the way to do that is to make the kids' learning visible and accountable." I couldn't agree with Bette more, and I know that the tools in this book can help you to do that kind of work.

Wrap Up

The only point of any learning activity must be to develop new thinking skills and processes that learners can use more independently and with more facility the next time they undertake that same challenge. That has been my aim: to give you tools that you can give your students, so that both of you can be more successful in your work— you at teaching and your students at learning.

And yet the best teaching *is* a form of learning. That has been the point of the teacher-research subtheme to this book. When we give students tools to make their thinking and reading visible, we can learn from students what they know, how they best learn, and what they need to be helped with next. This makes us better, more responsive, and more professional teachers.

As we engage in this process of observing students and their work, we become reflective practitioners, asking how students learn and how we can help them with their questions and challenges. We observe students so that we can engage them, providing them with the tools they need to do the work they need to do. This is strategic teaching.

Teacher research shifts the relationships in a classroom. Instead of delivering information, we invest ourselves in the creative and relational work of engaging, challenging, and assisting students in new ways—ways that help them meet the CCSS and the challenges facing them in their lives and the world. As we do so, we can provide students with tools such as those presented here, that can help them to undertake new relationships as well—with the content they are learning, with themselves as learners, with each other, and with the world. All of this happens when we shift our emphasis from "schoolishness" to "toolishness," from content to strategies, from information to knowledge construction, from ourselves to those we are trying to teach. I hope this book can help you to pursue this all-important work.

Bibliography

Works Cited

Applebee, A. (1993). Literature in the secondary school: Studies of curriculum and instruction in the United States. *NCTE Research Report No. 25*. Urbana, IL: National Council of Teachers of English.

Applebee, A. (1996). *Curriculum as conversation: Transforming traditions of teaching and learning*. Chicago: The University of Chicago Press.

Applebee, A. (1998). The teaching of literature in programs with reputations for excellence in English. Report Series 1.1. Albany, NY: Center for the Learning and Teaching of Literature. Microfiche.

Armstrong, T. (2003). *The multiple intelligences of reading and writing*. Alexandria, VA: ASCD.

Armstrong, T. (2000). *Multiple intelligences in the classroom*. Alexandria, VA: ASCD.

Armstrong, T. (1999). *Seven kinds of smart*. New York: Plume.

Barclay, K. D. (1990). Constructing meaning: An integrated approach to teaching reading. *Intervention in School and Clinic* 26.2: 84-91.

Baumann, J. (1986). The direct instruction of main idea comprehension ability. In J. F. Baumann (ed.), *Teaching main idea comprehension*, pp. 133–178. Newark, DE: International Reading Association.

Baumann, J. (1992). Teaching comprehension strategies. In B. L. Hayes (ed.), *Effective strategies for teaching reading*, pp. 61–83. Needham Heights, MA: Allyn & Bacon.

Baumann, J., Jones, L. & Seifert-Kessell, N. (1993). Monitoring reading comprehension by thinking aloud. *Instructional Resource Number 1*. Universities of Georgia and Maryland: National Reading Research Center.

Beach, R. & Myers, J. (2001). *Inquiry-based English instruction: Engaging students in life and literature*. New York: Teachers College Press.

Beach, R. & Appleman, D. (1984). Reading strategies for expository and literary text types. National Society for the Study of Education Yearbook.

Beck, I., McKeown, M. & Hamilton, R. (1997). *Questioning the author*. Newark, DE: International Reading Association.

Beck, I. & McKeown, M. (2006). *Improving comprehension with Questioning the Author*. New York: Scholastic.

Beers, K. (2002). *When kids can't read: What teachers can do*. Portsmouth, NH: Heinemann.

Bell, N. (1991). *Visualizing and verbalizing for language comprehension and thinking*. San Luis Obispo, CA: Nancibell Inc.

Bloom, B. (1976). *Human characteristics and school learning*. New York: McGraw-Hill.

Bloom, B. (Ed.). (1985). *Developing talent in young people*. New York: Ballantine.

Bolter, J. D. (1991). Writing space: *The computer, hypertext, and the history of writing*. Hillsdale, NJ: Lawrence Erlbaum.

Brown, J., Collins, A. & Duguid, P. (1989). Situated cognition and the culture of learning. *Educational Researcher, 18*(1) 32–42.

Bruner, J. (1986). *Actual minds, possible worlds*. Cambridge, MA: Harvard University Press.

Campbell, J., Voelkl, K. & Donahue, P. (1998). NAEP Trends in Academic Progress. Achievement of U.S. Students in Science, 1969 to 1996; Mathematics, 1973 to 1996; Reading, 1971 to 1996; Writing, 1984 to 1996." Washington DC: ED Publications.

Clyde, J., Barber, S., Hogue, S. & Wasz, L. (2006). *Breakthrough to meaning*. Portsmouth, NH: Heinemann.

Collins, A., Brown, J. & Newman, S. (1992). Cognitive apprenticeship: Teaching the crafts of reading, writing, and mathematics. In Resnick, L.B. (ed.), *Knowing, learning and instruction: Essays in honor of Robert Glaser*. Hillsdale, NJ: Lawrence Erlbaum.

Davey, B. (1983). Think aloud: Modeling the cognitive processes of reading comprehension. *Journal of Reading*. v27, n1, pp. 44–47.

Dweck, C. (2006). *Mindset: The new psychology of success*. New York: Random House.

Earl, L. (2003). *Assessment as learning: Using classroom assessment to maximize student learning*. Thousand Oaks, CA, Corwin Press.

Edmiston, B. (1991). What have you travelled? A teacher research study of structuring drama for reflection. Unpublished doctoral dissertation. Columbus, OH: The Ohio State University.

Fredericks, A. D. (1986). Mental imagery activities to improve comprehension. *Reading Teacher* 40, 78–81.

Frey, N. and Fisher, D. (2004). Using graphic novels, anime, and the Internet in an urban high school. *English Journal*, 93(3), 19–25.

Gambrell, L.B., & Koskinen, P.S. (2002). Imagery: A strategy for enhancing comprehension. In Block, C. C. & Pressley, M. (eds.), *Comprehension instruction: Research-based practices* (pp. 305–318). New York: Guilford.

Graue, M.E. (1993). *Ready for what? Constructing meanings of readiness for kindergarten.* Albany: SUNY Press.

Harvey, S. and A. Goudvis. (2000). *Strategies that work.* Portland, ME: Stenhouse.

Heathington, B. (1979). What to do about reading motivation in middle school. *Journal of Reading, 22,* pp. 709–713.

Hillocks, G., McCabe, B. & McCampbell, J. (1971). *The dynamics of English instruction, grades 7–12.* New York: Random House.

Hillocks, G. (1980). Toward a hierarchy of skills in the comprehension of literature. *English Journal 3*: pp. 601–612.

Hillocks, G. (1986). The writer's knowledge: Theory, research and implications for practice. In Bartholomae, D. & Petrosky, A. (eds.), *The 85th yearbook of the National Society for the Study of Education: The teaching of writing*, pp. 71–94. Chicago: University of Chicago Press.

Hillocks, G. & Smith, M. (1988). Sensible sequencing: Developing knowledge about literature text by text. *English Journal 77* (6): pp. 44–49.

Hillocks, G. (1995). *Teaching writing as reflective practice.* New York: Teachers College Press.

Hillocks, G. (1999). *Ways of thinking/ways of teaching.* New York: Teachers College Press.

Hillocks, G. (2001). *The testing trap.* New York: Teachers College Press.

Hughes, J., King, A., Perkins, P. & Fuke, V. (2011). Adolescents and "autobiographies": Reading and writing coming of age graphic novels. *Journal of Adolescent Literacy,* 54(8), 601–612.

Kamler, B. (2001). *Relocating the personal: A critical writing pedagogy.* Albany, NY: State University of New York Press.

Kohn, A. (1996). *Beyond discipline: From compliance to community.* Alexandria, VA: ASCD.

Lave, J. & Wenger, E. (1991). *Situated learning: Legitimate peripheral participation.* New York: Cambridge University Press.

Lehrer, R. (1993). Authors of knowledge: Patterns of hypermedia design. In Derry, S. & Lajoie, D. (eds.), *Computers as cognitive tools*, pp. 197–227. Hillsdale, NY: Lawrence Erlbaum.

McKenna, M., Ellsworth, R. & Kear, D. (1995). Children's attitudes towards reading: A national survey. *Reading Research Quarterly, 30,* pp. 934–957.

Medina, J. (2008). *Brain rules.* Seattle: Pear Press.

Meek, M. (1983). *Achieving literacy: Longitudinal studies of adolescents learning to read.* London: Kegan Paul.

Myers, M. (1996). *Changing our minds: Negotiating English and literacy.* Urbana, IL: NCTE.

National Assessment of Educational Progress. (1981). Reading, thinking, and writing: Results from the 1979-80 National Assessment of Reading and Literature. Denver: National Educational Commission of the States.

Newman, F. & Wehlage, G. (1995). *Successful school restructuring: A report to the public and educators by the Center on Organization and Restructuring of Schools.* Madison, WI: Wisconsin Center for Education Research.

Newman, F. & Associates. (1996). *Authentic achievement: Restructuring of schools for intellectual quality.* San Francisco: Jossey-Bass.

Nystrand, M. with Gamoran, A., Kachur, R. & Prendergast, C. (1997). *Opening dialogue: Understanding the dynamics of language and learning in the English classroom.* New York: Teachers College Press.

Ogle, D. (1983). K-W-L plus: A strategy for comprehension and summarization. *Journal of Reading 30*: pp. 626–631.

Paivio, A. (1986). *Mental representations.* New York: Oxford University Press.

Perkins, D. (2001). *Making learning whole.* San Francisco: Jossey-Bass.

Pink, D. (2011). *Drive: The surprising truth about what motivates us.* New York: Penguin.

Postman, N. (1996). *The ends of education... and how to get there.* CEE keynote at NCTE Spring meeting, Boston, MA: March 21.

Pressley, M. & Afflerbach, P. (1995). *Verbal protocols of reading: The nature of constructively responsive reading.* Hillsdale, NJ: Lawrence Erlbaum.

Rabinowitz, P. & Smith, M. (1998). *Authorizing readers: Resistance and respect in the teaching of literature.* New York: Teachers College Press.

Raphael, T. (1982). Question-answering strategies for children. *Reading Teacher* (36)2, pp. 186–190.

Rogoff, B., Matusov, B. & White, S. (1996). Models of teaching and learning: Participation in a community of learners. In Olson, D. & Torrance, N. (eds.), *The handbook of cognition and human development.* Oxford, UK: Blackwell.

Rosenblatt, L. (1978). *The reader, the text, the poem.* Carbondale, IL: Southern Illinois University Press.

Sadoski, M. (1985). The natural use of imagery in story comprehension and recall: Replication and extension. *Reading Research Quarterly* 20.5 (1985): pp. 658–667.

Shapiro, J. & White, W. (1991). Reading attitudes and perceptions in traditional and nontraditional reading programs. *Reading Research and Instruction*, 30, pp. 52–66.

Shepard, L. (2000). The role of assessment in a learning culture. *Educational Researcher*, Vol. 29, No. 7, pp. 4–14.

Smagorinsky, P. & Smith, M. (1992). The nature of knowledge in composition and literary understanding: A question of specificity. *Review of Educational Research*. 62, pp. 279–306.

Smagorinsky, P. (1991). *Expressions: Multiple intelligences in the English class*. Urbana, IL: NCTE.

Smith, F. (1978). *Joining the literacy club: Further essays into education*. Portsmouth, NH: Heinemann.

Smith, M. (1987). Teaching the interpretation of irony in poetry. *Research in the Teaching of English* 23.3: pp. 254–272.

Smith, M. (1991). *Understanding unreliable narrators*. Urbana, IL: NCTE.

Smith. M. (1998). Teaching argument: A workshop presented to the Maine Writing Project. July 2.

Smith, M. & Wilhelm. J. (2002). *Reading don't fix no Chevys: Literacy in the lives of young men*. Portsmouth, NH: Heinemann.

Smith, M. & Wilhelm, J. (2006). *Going with the flow: How to engage boys (and girls) in their literacy learning*. Portsmouth, NH: Heinemann.

Smith, M. & Wilhelm, J. (2007). *Getting it right: Fresh approaches to teaching grammar, usage, and correctness*. New York: Scholastic.

Smith, M. & Wilhelm, J. (2010). *Fresh takes on teaching the literary elements*. New York: Scholastic.

Stauffer, R. (1980). *Directing the reading-thinking process*. New York: Harper and Row.

Sulzby, E. (1985). Children's emergent reading of favorite storybooks: A developmental Study" *Reading Research Quarterly* 20.4.

Taylor, B., Harris, L., Pearson, P. & Garcia, G. (1995). *Reading difficulties, instruction, and assessment* (2nd ed.). New York: McGraw-Hill.

Tharp, R. & Gallimore, R. (1988). *Rousing minds to life: Teaching, learning, and schooling in social context*. Cambridge, UK: Cambridge University Press.

Vygotsky, L. (1962, 1978). *Mind in society: The development of higher psychological processes*. Cambridge, MA: Harvard University Press.

Wells, G. (1999). *Dialogic inquiry: Toward a sociocultural practice and theory of education*. New York: Cambridge University Press.

Whitin, P. (1996). *Sketching stories, stretching minds*. Portsmouth, NH: Heinemann.

Wiggins, G. & McTighe, J. (2001). *Understanding by design*. Alexandria, VA: ASCD.

Wilhelm, J. (1997/2008). *You gotta BE the book: Teaching engaged and reflective reading with adolescents*. New York: Teachers College Press.

Wilhelm, J. (2002/2012). *Action strategies for deepening comprehension* (2nd ed.). New York: Scholastic.

Wilhelm, J. (2004). *Reading IS seeing*. New York: Scholastic.

Wilhelm, J. (2007). *Engaging readers and writers with inquiry*. New York: Scholastic.

Wilhelm, J. & Novak, B. (2012). *Teaching literacy for love and wisdom: Being the book and being the change*. New York: Teachers College Press.

Wilhelm, J., Wilhelm, P. & Boas, E. (2009). *Inquiring minds learn to read and write*. Oakville, ONT: Rubicon.

Wilhelm, J., Baker, T. & Dube-Hackett, J. (2001). *Strategic reading: Guiding students to lifelong literacy*. Portsmouth, NH: Heinemann.

Wilhelm, J. & Edmiston, B. (1998). *Imagining to learn: Inquiry, ethics and integration through drama*. Portsmouth, NH: Heinemann.

Wilhelm, J. & Friedemann, P. (1998). *Hyperlearning: Where projects, inquiry, and technology meet*. York, ME: Stenhouse.

Wilhelm, J., Smith, M., Fredricksen, J. (2012). *Five Kinds of Knowledge/Five Kinds of Reading and Composing: Teaching Exposition*. Portsmouth, NH: Heinemann.

Wood, D., Bruner, J. & Ross, G. (1976). The role of tutoring in problem solving. *Journal of Child Psychiatry and Psychology*, 17(2), 89–100.

Wright, B., Betteridge, D. & Buckby, M. (1984). *Games for language learning*. Cambridge, UK: Cambridge University Press, 1984.

Index

E

Eisner, Elliot, 20
Engaging Readers and Writers with Inquiry (Wilhelm), 8
Expressions (Smagorinsky), 160

F

Feight, Gary, 41
"First Deer" (Corrigan), 12
firsthand experiences, 76–77
Fleischman, Paul, 184
floor plans/setting maps, 168
floorstorming, 77, 83–84, 92, 125
flow charts, 135, 160
Fontself, 133
formative assessments, 193–201
Fresh Takes on Teaching the Literary Elements (Smith and Wilhelm), 14
Friedman, Paul, 161, 174
From Pictures to Words: A Book About Making a Book (Stevens), 162
frontloading, 9, 74–82, 122, 125
frustration learning levels, 32

G

Gallimore, Ronald, 77
Gambrell, Linda B., 36
games, 58
Games for Language Learning (Wright, Bettridge and Buckby), 55
George, Jean Craighead, 67
Gliffy, 135
goals, identifying, 39–40
Goldenbock, Peter, 20
grab bags, 94–95
graphic novels, 68, 69
graphs, 135
Graue, Beth, 199
Great Fire, The (Murphy), 69, 70
Greenberg, Jan, 69, 151
guided imagery, read-alouds and, 163–164

H

Heller, Kristy, 191
Hess, Richard, 112–113
Hesse, Karen, 68
heuristics, 44–45, 103
Hillocks, George, 100, 140
historical inquiry, 46
historical texts, 161
humorous texts, 9
Hutchison, Katie, 145

I

I Know Why the Caged Bird Sings (Angelou), 187
illustrated texts, studying, 162–163

illustrating texts, 162–163
Imagechef, 130
imagery, 21, 53–54
Imagining to Learn (Wilhelm), 141
iMovie, 161
independent learning levels, 31
inferencing. *See* summarizing and inferencing
information gap activity, 55
information-transmission theory, 30, 199
information *vs.* knowledge, 27–28, 30, 102, 176–177
inquiry
    classroom inquiry, 175–176
    defined, 8, 42–43, 86
    heuristic *vs.* algorithmic thinking and, 44–45, 103
    historical inquiry, 46
importance of, 39, 43, 47
    knowledge *vs.* information, 27–28, 30, 102, 176–177
    visualization as, 45–46
inquiry frameworks, 19, 164–166, 175
Inspiration (website), 130
instructional learning levels, 31, 32
irony. *See* symbolism and irony
"issue treeing," 130

J

"joint productive activity," 30

K

knowledge *vs.* information, 27–28, 30, 102, 176–177
known to new teaching, 33–35, 72–74, 105
Koskinen, Patricia S., 36
K-W-L-(H) activity, 83

L

Langer, Judith, 70
language development. *See* vocabulary development
Lear, Edward, 116–117
learning-centered teaching
    apprenticeship teaching and, 30–31, 40
    "content knowledge," 103
    information-centered *vs.*, 27–28, 30, 102, 176–177
    inquiry frame, 19, 175
    overview, 27–43
    sequencing and, 100–103
    Vygotskian teaching theories and, 27, 31, 43, 76, 186
    see also sequencing
learning levels, 31–32
learning/reading biographies, 191
Learning Through Collaborative Visualization (CoVis), 46
learning transactions, 30

Lehrer, Rich, 28, 175, 176
Leon's Story (Tillage), 60–62
Levine, Alan, 127
literacy
    boys and, 71
    importance of, 48–49
LovelyCharts, 130

M

macro *vs.* micro goals, 39–40
main ideas
    definition, 108
    identifying in visual texts, 21, 111–112
    in poems, 113–114
    reading for (sample sequence), 108–111
    sequences for finding, 109–111
    symbolic border/picture frames, 190
    visual text, identifying in, 111–113
    writing summaries and, 114
main-idea tableaux, 19–20, 21
Manchester, Bette, 201
maps and mapping
mindmaps, 130
    tableaux maps, 160–161
    See also picture mapping
meaning
    in learning-centered teaching, 29
    word-level visualization for, 53–58
    See also character, understanding
Medina, John, 6
Meek, Margaret, 19, 68
mental modeling, 45–46, 60–63
Merow, Brooke, 87, 169
metacognitive awareness, 9, 118, 199
mindmaps, 130
MindMeister, 135
Morrill, George, 157
multimedia and technology
    in assignment sequences and projects, 131–136
    for frontloading/floorstorming, 125
    for multimodal composing, 128–129
    for murals and mapping, 130
    overview, 123–124
    for personality profiles, 143–145
    for visualizing text details and summarizing, 127–128
    for vocabulary development, 125–126
    wikis, 130, 131, 134
multimodal composing, 128–129
multi-modal essays, 134
Multiple Intelligence of Reading and Writing, The (Armstrong), 58
multisensory learning, 6
murals, multimedia, 130
Museum Box, 129
Myers, Miles, 27
Myers, Walter Dean, 161
My Side of the Mountain (George), 67
My Storymaker, 127